SACRAMENTO PUBLIC LIBRARY
828 "I" Street
Sacramento, CA 95814
04/18

D0782897

God's Word and You

Think

Ask

Bible

God's Word and You

What the Bible Says about Family,
Friends and other Important Stuff

Laura Martin

CF4·K

Copyright © Laura Martin 2016

10 9 8 7 6 5 4 3 2 1

Paperback ISBN: 978-1-78191-821-0

e-pub ISBN: 978-1-937-8

mobi ISBN: 978-1-78191-938-5

First published in 2016 by

Christian Focus Publications Ltd,

Geanies House, Fearn, Ross-shire

IV20 1TW, Scotland

www.christianfocus.com

Cover and internal page design by Pete Barnsley (Creativehoot.com)

Printed and bound by Bell and Bain, Glasgow

MIX
Paper from
responsible sources
FSC® C007785

"Scripture quotations are from The ESV®Bible (The Holy Bible, English Standard Version®), published by HarperCollinsPublishers, ©2001 by Crossway. Used by permission. All rights reserved."

All rights reserved. No part of this publication may be reproduced, stored in a retrieval system, or transmitted, in any form, by any means, electronic, mechanical, photocopying, recording or otherwise without the prior permission of the publisher or a licence permitting restricted copying. In the U.K. such licences are issued by the Copyright Licensing Agency, Saffron House, 6-10 Kirby Street, London, EC1 8TS. www.cla.co.uk

FROM THE AUTHOR TO YOU

My name is Laura Martin and I'm married to Bryan. We have five beautiful children and a crazy spaniel. I serve alongside my husband, who is pastor of River City Bible Church – a church we planted in Hamilton, New Zealand in 2010. Prior to that we were serving in a church in the U.K. I home-school our children, enjoy travelling, gardening, quilting, projects around the house, and writing. I love to disciple and counsel from God's precious Word. Thank you for reading!

Laura Martin

You can contact Laura at: laureemartin75@gmail.com

Dedication

For our precious children,

Georgia, Lucy, Jack, Kate and Will

You are the very reason that I write these books.

My heart longs for you to know that Scripture is sufficient for every question.

May Jesus satisfy you always, may His Word be the Bread of Life to your souls, and may you grow to be women and men who love and proclaim the gospel – all for His glory.

I love you all so much!

Mama

And for Bryan.

My best friend.

Because of you, I can.

Lauree x

Contents

What does the Bible say about ...?

What does the
Bible Say about...

Friendship?

Think

Ask

Bible

There was once a friendship formed between two very unlikely young men. One was a shepherd, the other was the son of a king. The shepherd boy was the youngest of a large God-fearing family and the prince was the son of a kingdom's first-ever king. One boy was hidden away from the public eye, tending to his father's sheep; the other was raised in pomp and ceremony, in training to one day succeed his father's throne. It seems an unlikely connection, doesn't it? How would two such young men even meet?

Well, their meeting was in fact very memorable. I wonder if you have already guessed who these lads are? One more clue, just in case. Think: giant and slingshot. Yes! You've got it; we are talking about David and Jonathan. Not only was their first meeting memorable but it formed the beginning of a beautiful and perhaps unique friendship. Why would I say unique? Well, I think that how the Bible describes this wonderful friendship is a lot different from how the world would describe friendship. So let's have a look at the three main characters whose lives unfold before us in the book of 1 Samuel. This will help us to see exactly what made this friendship so amazing, and how God used this friendship to achieve His purposes.

David

David was the shepherd-boy-turned-soldier-turned king! He was the son of Jesse the Bethlehemite. One of the neat things that we know about Jesse is that he was the grandson of Ruth and Boaz (see the book of Ruth in the Old Testament). In fact, were you to read the genealogy (family tree) in the gospel of Matthew, chapter 1, you would see that David is in Jesus' family tree. Isn't that amazing!

Anyway, as we know, David worked in the family business looking after his father's sheep. In New Zealand where I live, a shepherd's task isn't too dangerous compared to being a shepherd in Israel. In Israel, in

Bible times, there were wild animals like lions, bears and wolves, who would happily pick off one or two sheep for their dinner! This meant David had to be very skilled in protecting the sheep. In David's day, there were no rifles to kill wild animals, but he did have a slingshot. Can you see already how God was using David's role as a shepherd to train him for being a soldier in the future?

But there is something else about David. David was chosen by God to replace Saul as king. As you will soon see, Saul was not a king who obeyed God, so God chose a man who loved Him to be the next king: that man was David. David did not know when or even how he would be crowned king, but he trusted God and continued to serve right where he was, as a shepherd, until God made him king.

Just one more thing about David: he was a man who loved God. In fact, God even calls David 'a man after my own heart' (Acts 13:22). David loved to worship God by writing songs and playing the harp. Many of the songs he wrote are recorded for us in the Book of Psalms in the Old Testament. Why don't you take some time to read Psalm 23, written by David the shepherd. He uses his life as a shepherd as a picture of God's care for His people, referring to God as his Shepherd and the people as His sheep. Isn't that beautiful?

But back to the king thing … why would God want David to be king? Was King Saul really doing such a bad job? Read on and see…

Did You Know ...?

A theocracy is a system of government where God is the head of State and His Word is law. Israel was under a theocracy from the time of Moses to the time of Samuel, when Saul was made king.

Saul

Before the kingdom of Israel had a king, they had judges who spoke to the people on behalf of God and helped to govern and lead the people. The people were governed under a theocracy.

A prophet called Samuel was the Judge of Israel when Saul was a young man. You might remember Samuel as the much-wanted child of the woman Hannah, who for many years was unable to have a baby. The Lord answered Hannah's prayer for a child and in return she gave Samuel to the Lord for His service, allowing the child to live with and be an assistant to the judge of the time, Eli. Sadly, Eli's sons did not follow the Lord, so God raised up Samuel to take over from Eli after Eli's death. Samuel was a good judge over Israel, but when he became old and his sons became judges, they did not fear the Lord either. Instead of allowing God to deal with these men His way, the Israelite people decided they just wanted a human king instead so they could be like the other nations. This meant they were rejecting God as their king. God warned the people against having a human king to rule over them (you can read this warning in 1 Samuel 8:10-22). However, the people were insistent so God gave them their king. Enter stage right: Saul.

Saul was known as a very handsome man and in fact he was also a very tall man, being at least a head taller than anyone else (1 Samuel 9:2). Sadly, we do not read anything about Saul being a God-fearing man, but we do read in 1 Samuel 10:9 that God gave Saul another heart, equipping him for the very sacred role ahead. Saul was not devoted to the Lord. And sadly it was not long before Saul was dishonouring the Lord by following his own ways instead of God's ways. God was patient with Saul but even so, Saul's consistent sin meant that God eventually rejected him as king and chose David for the job instead.

And Samuel said to Saul, 'I will not return with you. For you have rejected the word of the LORD, and the LORD has rejected you from being king over Israel.' As Samuel turned to go away, Saul seized the skirt of his robe, and it tore. And Samuel said to him, 'The LORD has torn the kingdom of Israel from you this day and has given it to a neighbour of yours, who is better than you.'

—1 Samuel 15:26-28

Saul did not know who the man was or when this new king would reign, but it soon became apparent that David was a threat to him. Saul, consumed with jealousy and hatred, made many attempts to take David's life. Saul in his sin was trying to protect his role as king. However, Satan was also at work, trying to get rid of David in order to keep Israel without a God-fearing king, and to stop David's line of descendants, which would eventually lead to Jesus. Satan was using Saul's sin of selfishness to try to stop Jesus being born! Sin is serious!

Jonathan

From our first glimpse of Jonathan in 1 Samuel 14 we see that Jonathan believed in the Lord. In fact, the Lord used Jonathan's simple and genuine faith in Him to save Israel from the Philistines. Jonathan was a stark contrast to his father, Saul. While Saul was making rash decisions, Jonathan was working in the background, being used by God often to thwart his father's foolish behaviour. Jonathan even stepped aside from his rightful succession to his father's throne and submitted willingly to God's plan for David. Jonathan was a selfless young man. But don't be tempted to think this young man was a sissy. He was a mighty warrior and athlete. Don't forget that he was next in line to the throne and much of his life would have been in training for this role, which includes being a mighty and skilled warrior. Jonathan was loved and respected by the people. We see this in 1 Samuel 14 when Jonathan and his armour-bearer were near the Philistine camp. Jonathan believed that the Lord would give him victory over the Philistines that day and so he told his armour bearer to come with him to fight. Now think about this: There were many Philistines. There were two Israelites. But the armour- bearer's response to Jonathan tells us of his great love for his master. He said, 'Do all that is in your heart. Do as you wish. Behold, I am with you heart and soul.' (1 Samuel 14:7). Jonathan was brave and courageous and his love for the people of Israel was evident in his willingness to put his life on the line for their protection.

So now we know a little more about the three characters we'll be looking at in our study of Jonathan and David's friendship. And where did Jonathan and David meet? At the battle line, where, for many days, the Israelites had been tormented by a huge Philistine called Goliath. Not one man was prepared to fight this giant man. Until, that is, David came from the fields to deliver food to his soldier brothers. That's when he ended up killing Goliath with his slingshot and a stone.

Jonathan, of course, had watched this situation unfold.

The Philistine said to David, 'Come to me and I will give your flesh to the birds of the air and to the beasts of the field.' Then David said to the Philistine, 'You come to me with a sword and with a spear and with a javelin, but I come to you in the name of the LORD of hosts, the God of the armies of Israel, whom you have defied. This day the LORD will deliver you into my hand, and I will strike you down and cut off your head. And I will give the dead bodies of the host of the Philistines this day to the birds of the air and to the wild beasts of the earth, that all the earth may know that there is a God in Israel, and that all this assembly may know that the LORD saves not with sword and spear. For the battle is the LORD's, and he will give you into our hand.'

—1 Samuel 17:44-47

After David had succeeded in killing Goliath, you can imagine the shout of celebration and victory that came from the Israelites. They had been freed from the hold of this Philistine!

What happened next? When David was summoned to speak with the king, what would the king's son have felt? Jealousy? Admiration? Let's see …

As soon as he was finished speaking to Saul, the soul of Jonathan was knit to the soul of David, and Jonathan loved him as his own soul.

—1 Samuel 18:1

Jonathan loved David. This is the key to their amazing friendship – selfless love. Jonathan saw David come and defeat the enemy that neither he nor his father nor the rest of the Israelite army could defeat, and yet, instead of feeling intimidated, envious or even a little annoyed that a mere shepherd did better than any mighty warrior, Jonathan loved him. Jonathan also gave David his robe, his armour, his belt, his sword – all that he himself would wear as a mighty warrior. And you can bet that it wasn't the common armour that every other soldier would have had. No, it was the armour of a prince. What Jonathan was doing was clothing David as a prince, allowing David the highest honour that anyone could have in the king's court. Remembering that the eldest prince was the one who was heir to the throne, Jonathan unknowingly clothed David correctly because it would in fact be David and not Jonathan who would one day become king. Jonathan put David above himself by de-robing himself for David.

As we read through Samuel, the plot of jealous hatred unfolds with numerous accounts of David serving Saul in his army, playing the harp to ease Saul's troubled mind and then fleeing from Saul in order to preserve his life. All the while, Jonathan is in the background, watching his father become murderous towards his dearest friend. What a terrible position that Jonathan is placed in, having to slyly help David in hiding, while still serving on the battlefield with his father. But Jonathan loved David. Can you see some opposites here? Love caused Jonathan to work hard for David's best interests, while jealous hatred caused Saul to work hard for his own best interests.

But wait, there's more!

What other Principles can we Learn from Scripture?

Bible

We can all try our hardest, even with the Lord's help to be the kind of friend that Jonathan was to David, but I promise you that there will be times we fail. Sometimes we will say or do things that we regret; sometimes we will act selfishly or unkindly. Sometimes our friends will not treat us the way we want to be treated. This is all because of sin. But Jesus can help us to be the kind of friend that Jonathan was to David. If we are truly saved, if we believe that Jesus is our Saviour, the Holy Spirit will live within us and He will begin to transform us so that we become more like Jesus.

But the fruit of the Spirit is love, joy, peace, patience, kindness, goodness, faithfulness, gentleness, self-control.

—Galatians 5:22-23

▼ *more...*

The fruit of the Spirit, as described in the previous verse, is what we should see in the lives of all Christians because the Holy Spirit lives within all believers and transforms them.

What did we Learn about Friendship?

Ask

1. Selfless love in a friendship crosses cultural and social barriers.

2. Selfless love in a friendship leads us to rejoice with each other instead of becoming jealous.

3. Selfless love in a friendship is built on a common bond in the Lord.

4. Selfless love in a friendship leads us to encourage one another in the Lord.

5. Selfless love in a friendship leads us to want the best for our friend.

6. Selfless love leads to friends who have a lasting influence on us.

7. Selfless love in friendship is an opportunity for us to show the fruit of the Spirit in our lives.

Study Questions

1. How do you think the fruit of the Spirit would impact or change friendships?

   Think

2. Write out each 'fruit' and next to it, write a description of this fruit as it would look in friendship.

3. If you are a Christian, you and others should be able to see the fruit of the Spirit fairly consistently in your life. Are there any areas of your life that you need the Lord's help to develop more? We all need help with our lives. Sometimes we need different sorts of help depending on who we might be with.

4. How did Jesus show the fruit of the Spirit in His relationships with people? Give examples.

5. Can you think of other verses in the Bible that talk about the fruit mentioned in Galatians 5? If not, look some up from the concordance in the back of your Bible.

5. What are some practical ways that you can apply the fruit of the Spirit to some of your friendships this week?

Let's Pray Together

Dear God, thank you for Jonathan and David's friendship and the work you did in their hearts. Please enable me to be a friend who loves selflessly, preferring others above myself and rejoicing in their joys and weeping with them in their trials. Jesus, thank you for being the best friend that anyone could ever have. Thank you for paying the price for my sin and for allowing me to come into a right friendship with you. Please help me to tell others about you, the friend of sinners. Amen.

BUT THE FRUIT OF THE SPIRIT IS LOVE, JOY, PEACE, PATIENCE, KINDNESS, GOODNESS, FAITHFULNESS, GENTLENESS, SELF-CONTROL. (GALATIANS 5:22-23)

MY ACTION PLAN ...

1.

2.

3.

4.

5.

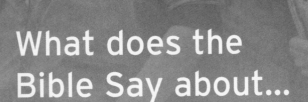

What does the Bible Say about...

Work?

Think

Ask

Bible

What does the word 'work' mean to you? You might use it to describe the thing that adults do so they can earn money. When our girls were younger they would sometimes say in the mornings, 'Daddy, why do you have to go to work?' He would teasingly reply, 'So that we can buy cookies!' There is an element of truth in that. Working earns us money so that our families can be provided for.

Work isn't always 'paid work', though. There are other kinds of work, like homework, housework, volunteer work. Sometimes 'work' of whatever sort means that we have to do things that we might not choose to do if it were up to us. But God, in His Bible, gives us instructions regarding work. Before we look at those instructions, let's look at someone who knew what it meant to work hard and to work for the Lord.

There was once a young man, relatively unknown to any but his own family and those around him who watched him. Now you might think it a bit strange that this young man would be watched, it's not like he was famous. But it's true. And as this young man went quietly and diligently about his work, he put his best effort into all that he did. God enabled this young man to be successful – so successful in fact that those who were watching him promoted him to a very significant, important and difficult role. And guess what? He continued to work hard and he continued to prosper in all that he did.

You might be thinking, 'So what? Plenty of people work hard and are rewarded for their efforts.' That would be true. But this young guy's story is vastly different to any we might hear about today. Let me clue you in. The young man's name was Joseph and what makes his story so noteworthy was the extremely difficult circumstances that he faced every day. These circumstances might have hampered you or me, but somehow, the harder Joseph's situation became, the more incentive it gave him to do his best.

Perhaps you will remember Joseph as the teenager sold to Egyptian slave traders by his own brothers. He was seventeen years old at the time and, if truth be known, he was a bit spoilt. It seemed he pushed his brothers over the edge one day when he told them a dream he had that involved them (the older brothers) bowing down to him (the annoying younger brother).

So, off Joseph went to Egypt, likely tied behind a camel for a long, long walk. But Joseph trusted God.

Fast forward about thirteen years. Joseph is now about thirty and is a slave in Potiphar's household. Potiphar was one of Pharaoh's officers. The Lord caused Joseph to succeed in all that he did in Potiphar's house. But what exactly was it that Joseph did? He probably performed household tasks for Potiphar and his wife: things like serving food and drinks to his master and mistress. They certainly wouldn't have been tasks that Joseph would have chosen to do, but he did them diligently and the Lord blessed his attitude.

Now Joseph had been brought down to Egypt, and Potiphar, an officer of Pharaoh, the captain of the guard, an Egyptian, had bought him from the Ishmaelites who had brought him down there. The Lord was with Joseph, and he became a successful man, and he was in the house of his Egyptian master. His master saw that the Lord was with him and that the Lord caused all that he did to succeed in his hands. So Joseph found favour in his sight and attended him, and he made him overseer of his house and put him in charge of all that he had. From the time that he made him overseer in his house and over all that he had the Lord blessed the Egyptian's house for Joseph's sake; the blessing of the Lord was on all that he had, in house and field. So he left all that he had in Joseph's charge, and because of him he had no concern about anything but the food he ate.

—Genesis 39:1-6

Did You Know ...?

People could become slaves if they couldn't pay back debt.
Think very carefully before you borrow anything!

So let's think this through. Joseph was sold to Potiphar as a slave. Can you imagine the panic Joseph must have felt to be handed over to Potiphar's charge and expected to work hard with little to no chance of knowing his own freedom again? And if he didn't work hard he could expect to be beaten, or even worse. He was never free to do as he wished or even to contact his family and let them know what had happened. He was stuck. Yet Joseph worked hard and saw great reward for it.

But then, disaster struck. Joseph was wrongly accused and jailed. He was out of sight and out of mind of any who might be in a position to help him. But God, in His great love for Joseph, provided a way of release. In fact, Joseph was not only released but he was given a position of great power in Pharaoh's kingdom.

How did this happen? How can someone go from the dungeons of a prison to being a powerful man in Pharoah's kingdom? Especially a guy who is not even an Egyptian, but an Israelite.

Well, Pharaoh had a strange dream ...

After two whole years, Pharaoh dreamed that he was standing by the Nile, and behold, there came up out of the Nile seven cows attractive and plump, and they fed in the reed grass. And behold, seven other cows, ugly and thin, came up out of the Nile after them, and stood by the other cows on the bank of the Nile. And the ugly, thin cows ate up the seven attractive, plump cows. And Pharaoh awoke. And he fell asleep and dreamed a second time. And behold, seven ears of grain, plump and good, were growing on one stalk. And behold, after them sprouted seven ears, thin and blighted by the east wind. And the thin ears swallowed up the seven plump, full ears. And Pharaoh awoke, and behold, it was a dream. So in the morning his spirit was troubled, and he sent and called for all the magicians of Egypt and all its wise men. Pharaoh told them his dreams, but there was none who could interpret them to Pharaoh.

—Genesis 41:1-8

Of course, when Pharaoh awoke he was troubled and called for the magicians and wise men of Egypt to interpret the dream. But they could not interpret it. Nobody could, until a man who had met Joseph in prison and had his own dream interpreted by Joseph, spoke up. Joseph was summoned to Pharaoh and through God's special enabling, gave Pharaoh God's message for him through his dream. Now look at what happens next. Pharaoh not only accepted Joseph's interpretation of the dream but he saw that God was using Joseph in an amazing way:

And Pharaoh said to his servants, 'Can we find a man like this, in whom is the Spirit of God?' Then Pharaoh said to Joseph, 'Since God has shown you all this, there is none so discerning and wise as you are. You shall be over my house, and all my people shall order themselves as you command. Only as regards the throne will I be greater than you.' And Pharaoh said to Joseph, 'See, I have set you over all the land of Egypt.'

—Genesis 41:38-41

What happened next? God gave Joseph more work. Harder work, more responsibility, more power, greater authority. But God knew Joseph was ready for it. Joseph had shown himself to be willing to work hard, even in the most difficult of circumstances. God gave Joseph opportunity to be diligent and to work hard, even in a foreign culture as a slave. And Joseph responded in the right way. Joseph was faithful to work hard and honour the Lord by his life. Even Pharaoh saw that.

The Bible tells us that Joseph went all over Egypt, storing food for the famine. And what's more, it seems that not once did he take for granted his freedom in Pharaoh's kingdom in order to escape and head back home. Joseph knew that God was using him for His own special purposes. What God was doing was a mystery to Joseph, but Joseph chose to trust God and to work hard for God's glory and purposes.

But wait, there's more!

What other Principles can we Learn from Scripture?

Bible

The Bible gives us a lot of wisdom about work. Let's just look at a few to get us started, but I know that in your own Bible readings it won't be long before you start to see Scriptures that apply to work.

1. Do it for the Lord.

The verse on the following page tells us that if we are Christians we are to do everything as if we were doing it for the Lord – this is the same attitude that Joseph displayed. In fact, the Bible even talks to slaves about their attitude to work. In many societies today, slavery is condemned and illegal. However, we can apply that same principle

▼ more...

to anyone doing a task for someone. That might be an employee in their place of work, a student doing work at school, a volunteer helping to plant trees in a local park or even a child who is doing chores at home. And if we are doing something for the Lord, then we do our very best with a cheerful and uncomplaining attitude.

Slaves, obey in everything those who are your earthly masters, not by way of eye-service, as people-pleasers, but with sincerity of heart, fearing the Lord. Whatever you do, work heartily, as for the Lord and not for men, knowing that from the Lord you will receive the inheritance as your reward. You are serving the Lord Christ.

—Colossians 3:22-24

2. Don't Fall into Laziness.

Did you know that laziness is a sin? It really is. But it's not so much the action of not making your bed or not completing a task properly, it's the attitude behind it. Often when we are lazy we have the 'I can't be bothered' attitude. Or the 'no one is going to care' attitude. Or maybe the 'I shouldn't have to do this' attitude. But as we have already seen from Colossians 3:22, our attitude towards work is as important as the carrying out of the actual task. Look again at Colossians 3:22. It tells us how not to work – 'not as people-pleasers, but with sincerity of heart, fearing the Lord.' What does that mean? To fear the Lord means that we have a reverent understanding of the holy and powerful God we serve and rightly fear Him out of respect and honour of who He is. The verse tells us that sincerity of heart in our attitudes towards our work flows out of the fear of God. Psalm 111:10 says, 'The fear of the LORD is the beginning of wisdom.'

▼ *more...*

20

Wisdom enables us to think and act wisely in our work. Even the ants work hard with wisdom as they work to store food for their needs. Laziness does not produce results, and neither does it honour the Lord. Be like the ant!

Go to the ant, O sluggard; consider her ways, and be wise. Without having any chief, officer, or ruler, she prepares her bread in summer and gathers her food in harvest. How long will you lie there, O sluggard? When will you arise from your sleep? A little sleep, a little slumber, a little folding of the hands to rest, and poverty will come upon you like a robber, and want like an armed man.

—Proverbs 6:6-11

What did we Learn about Work?

1. It is right to work hard at whatever task is before us … even if it is really hard for us to do!

2. God blesses those who are diligent to work hard.

3. We ought to be willing to do whatever tasks are before us, never thinking ourselves too 'good' to do them.

4. God is honoured by the person who works diligently in His name.

5. A good worker is a wonderful witness of God to others.

6. We need to work for the Lord.

7. We need to avoid the trap of laziness.

Study Questions

1. Read Proverbs 21:25 – *'The desire of the sluggard kills him, for his hands refuse to labour.'*
   - Give some ways in which the desires of the sluggard might kill him.

2. Read Proverbs 26:14-16 – *'As a door turns on its hinges, so does a sluggard on his bed. The sluggard buries his hand in the dish; it wears him out to bring it back to his mouth. The sluggard is wiser in his own eyes than seven men who can answer sensibly.*

- The sluggard is a man who gives up opportunities to be up and out the door, to work or be productive. However, it's clear that he likes comfort – the ability to dig his hand into a dish of food. But perhaps his extreme laziness has made him physically unable to carry out basic tasks like feeding himself, or maybe he is just pretending he can't feed himself so that he isn't obliged to do any more than that! And yet he thinks his way is best. He has worked out a lifestyle where he can stay in bed and not have to work! What might that say about other areas of his life that he might be lazy in? How do you think this lazy man (or woman!) would manage to keep a job? Or care for a family? What about showing love to others in serving them? Or even keeping up with personal hygiene? What would you say to this lazy man or woman?

3. Compare the sluggard to Jesus as He is described in Philippians 2: 5-9 – *'Have this mind among yourselves, which is yours in Christ Jesus, who, though he was in the form of God, did not count equality with God a thing to be grasped, but*

▼ *more...*

22

made himself nothing, taking the form of a servant, being born in the likeness of men, And being found in human form, he humbled himself by becoming obedient to the point of death, even death on a cross. Therefore God has highly exalted him and bestowed on him the name that is above every name.

- What attitudes did Jesus have as he carried out the task that His Heavenly Father had for Him to do?

- What are your attitudes to any sort of work or task that you have to do? Do they compare more to the sluggard or to Jesus' attitudes?

Let's Pray Together

Dear God, thank you for what we have learned about attitudes towards working that honour you. Thank you for the example of Joseph who, even in the midst of really awful circumstances, still did his best to honour you by being diligent and hard-working. Thank you also for Jesus, who showed us the best attitude towards any task. He is humble and kind and he sacrificed Himself for the benefit of all who would believe in Him. His work on the cross was the hardest work ever done, and yet He did it willingly for me. I pray that I would have the same attitudes towards any work or tasks that I am asked to do. Help me to honour you and please give me the strength and courage to be a hard worker. Amen.

SLAVES, OBEY IN EVERYTHING THOSE WHO ARE YOUR EARTHLY MASTERS, NOT BY WAY OF EYE-SERVICE, AS PEOPLE-PLEASERS, BUT WITH SINCERITY OF HEART, FEARING THE LORD. WHATEVER YOU DO, WORK HEARTILY, AS FOR THE LORD AND NOT FOR MEN, KNOWING THAT FROM THE LORD YOU WILL RECEIVE THE INHERITANCE AS YOUR REWARD. YOU ARE SERVING THE LORD CHRIST. (COLOSSIANS 3:22-24)

MY ACTION PLAN ...

1.

2.

3.

4.

5.

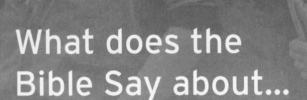

What does the Bible Say about...

Worry?

Think

Ask

Bible

Imagine this: You're at home, doing your thing; washing clothes, grinding flour to make bread, tending to animals, sweeping the house, gathering wood for the fire, hauling water from the well, trading goods and food. (Oh, did I mention that it's your normal day about 2,000 years ago?)

Suddenly, you hear a commotion. You run out to see and there's Jesus and His disciples! He is a dear friend and so what do you do? You insist He come and eat and lodge at your home, for as long as He needs to. That's just what Martha did. She was the sister of Mary and Lazarus, and might have been a widow because it seems she owned the home they all lived in. She certainly was a generous, hard-working and hospitable woman. Without hesitation, when the Lord turned up, Martha put aside her 'to do' list and made a completely new one. 'To do: serve the Lord and make sure He has a good meal.' And that is exactly what Martha set out to do.

Now remember back in those days there were no convenience stores, no convenience food, and, in fact, very little convenience at all. There were no freezers with meat ready to be defrosted and used for unexpected guests. Nope, animals would have been slaughtered and prepared right there and then. There were no store-bought loaves of bread for a quick sandwich, no packets of cookies or crackers, no microwaves to heat up a quick meal, no bags of pre-prepared salad anywhere ... it was all make from scratch, hard work. But Martha was a hard worker, so no problem there. Perhaps it wasn't too long, though, before Martha looked around her kitchen in a bit of panic, feeling the burden of the task ahead, when she suddenly realised her sister Mary wasn't there helping her! She popped her head around the door only to see Mary was in fact just sitting at Jesus' feet, listening to Him teach! Can you imagine what was going through Martha's mind? Maybe it was, 'I can't believe it! She knows how much work there is to do in order to have a meal ready for our Lord, and yet she has left it all up to me!' Whatever she thought, Martha was clearly frustrated. So Martha went straight to Jesus with her complaint:

Now as they went on their way, Jesus entered a village. And a woman named Martha welcomed him into her house. And she had a sister called Mary, who sat at the Lord's feet and listened to his teaching. But Martha was distracted with much serving. And she went up to him and said, 'Lord, do you not care that my sister has left me to serve alone? Tell her then to help me.'

—Luke 10:38-40

In our home we use the word 'miffed' to describe a response like Martha's. Martha was so 'miffed' that she actually interrupted Jesus as He taught, to complain that He did not care about her working alone in the kitchen! Uh oh! But wait, there's more … she then demanded that He tell Mary to get up and get out to the kitchen! Oh dear. Now, perhaps you might be thinking that what Martha was saying was reasonable. When someone turns up at your home unexpectedly and you want to provide food for them, it shouldn't be too unreasonable to expect that others in your home will help you. But there is a problem with that. Jesus isn't just any old person. He is the Son of God, who came to seek and to save the lost (Luke 19:10). Martha knew that. She was a believer. She would have known that He was the very same Jesus who recently provided food for thousands from two fish and five loaves of bread. Even without Facebook, news like that would have travelled fast!

So what was Jesus' response to poor old miffed Martha?

But the Lord answered her, 'Martha, Martha, you are anxious and troubled about many things, but one thing is necessary. Mary has chosen the good portion, which will not be taken away from her.'

—Luke 10:41-42

Jesus knew exactly what Martha's problem was. It wasn't that she didn't have enough help in the kitchen (because He who provides for all of our needs was right there in her home!) No, Martha's problem was that she was anxious and troubled. These are two words that describe worry.

Did You Know ...?

Doing the right thing at the wrong time is the wrong thing. Have a think about that ...

Perhaps you are wondering what Martha was worried about. Let's look again at what Jesus said to her, which will help us to see the issue.

Martha was worried about many things. This is understandable. There was a huge amount of work involved in preparing a meal and she would have felt pressure as she wanted it to be just perfect for the Lord she loved. She wanted to please the Lord by what she was doing. But therein lay her problem. She was doing the wrong thing.

Jesus pointed out that Mary had made the best choice. She had chosen to care for her soul. When given a choice over preparing a meal for Jesus,or having a few short hours to listen to His sweet voice feeding her soul, Mary knew it was a no-brainer. She went straight to His feet for a front row seat. Mary knew that Jesus' words were life-giving (John 6:63). She knew that Jesus Himself was the bread of life (John 6:35).

What are the words that Jesus used to describe Martha? He said she was 'anxious and troubled'. That's what happens to us too. Martha had allowed the situation around her to distract her from the reality that the Son of God was actually sitting in her home! He did not need her service to Him! She needed to hear His words.

We do that too, don't we? We allow the circumstances in our lives to distract us from Jesus' words, causing us to become anxious and troubled. But there is a simple answer. Sit at Jesus' feet (open your Bible) and listen to Jesus' life-giving words, which will feed your soul.

Martha asked the Lord a question. She said, 'Lord, do you not care …?' Do you think Martha really believed the Lord didn't care about her? I think deep down she knew He did, but worry can drag us down so much that sometimes we don't even think or act rationally. However, here's the answer we find to Martha's question, from the Bible.

Humble yourselves, therefore, under the mighty hand of God so that at the proper time he may exalt you, casting all your anxieties on him, because he cares for you.

—1 Peter 5:6-7

This is interesting. Before the above Scriptures even speak about worry, they speak of pride. Do you see that? The command to humble ourselves tells us that we need to stop relying on ourselves and instead rely on God. Often we worry because there is a situation out of our control that we wish we could control. Does that make sense? A maths test that you don't think you did very well in, or a trip to the dentist that you can't avoid, or a feeling that other kids are speaking unkindly about you, are perhaps things you might have felt worried about before. Or perhaps something is happening in our family that we don't like. But when you believe that ultimately God is in control of everything that happens in life, you can trust Him with everything, including all the things you feel worried about. Why can we trust God with our worries? Because, as the verse in 1 Peter tells us, He cares for us.

My frame was not hidden from you, when I was being made in secret, intricately woven in the depths of the earth. Your eyes saw my

unformed substance; in your book were written, every one of them, the
days that were formed for me, when as yet there were none of them.

—Psalm 139:15-16

These verses in Psalms show us God's care for us. He is the God who knew us before our bodies had even been formed. He knew what we would be good at, what we would struggle with, who our parents would be, what books we would like to read – all of these things He knew because of His great love for us. He cared for us before we were even born. The biggest show of His love for us is the provision of His Son, Jesus, to die on the cross and pay the penalty for our sin! Even though we were a couple of thousand years away from being born, God loved us so much that He provided a way back to Him from sin, through the death and resurrection of Jesus. Do you know this care of God for you? Have you responded to Him in faith and repentance?

What a wonderful blessing to know that we can cast our worries onto God who has cared for us from always. But when we do cast our worries on Him, what then? Does what we want just magically happen? Do we get an A in that maths test? No, not necessarily. The Bible does promise us something, though:

Do not be anxious about anything, but in everything by prayer and
supplication with thanksgiving let your requests be made known to
God. And the peace of God, which surpasses all understanding, will
guard your hearts and your minds in Christ Jesus.

—Philippians 4:6-7

Do You See what it is that the Bible Promises Us?

Once we have humbly cast our cares on the Lord, we will know God's peace. Phew! Worrying can feel so heavy and there is nothing like casting off that heaviness and having it replaced with peace. God is so kind to us! Look back at verse seven. What does the peace of God do for us? It will guard our minds and our hearts. You know how sometimes we can allow things in our minds to go round and round and round ... and we become more and more messed up about it. Well, God promises that His peace will guard our minds once we have cast our anxieties on Him. Here's the key, though. It's not a 'pray just once' kind of command. It's a 'pray continually' command. Every single time you are tempted towards worrying, cast that worry to Jesus in prayer, reminding yourself God is trustworthy and that He cares for you! Then allow the peace of God to guard your heart and mind.

But wait, there's more!

What other Principles can we Learn from Scripture?

Bible

Jesus told Martha that she was anxious and troubled about many things. There is something else we can learn from Martha's example. Martha's mind was unguarded. Do you know what that means? It means that she had allowed her mind to collect up things which were out of her control, so that she might worry about them. Do you do that? It's easy to do. There might be a whole bunch of little things which, when they are all added up, make us feel really worried. But here's an interesting thing to think about. Much of what we worry about hasn't yet happened, and possibly won't happen. And, here's another thing: even if it did happen, we couldn't do anything about it anyway.

And he [Jesus] said to his disciples, 'Therefore I tell you, do not be anxious about your life, what you will eat, nor about your body, what you will put on. For life is more than food, and the body more important than clothing. Consider the ravens: they neither sow nor reap, they have neither storehouse nor barn, and yet God feeds them. Of how much more value are you than the birds! And which of you by being anxious can add a single hour to his span of life? If then you are not able to do as small a thing as that, why are you anxious about the rest?'

—Luke 12:22-26

Jesus even had to remind His disciples of these truths. As He spoke to them, He knew that soon He would have to return to His Father in Heaven, leaving them to get on with the work He had equipped them for: taking the gospel to the world. While they had been with Him, He had been providing for all of their needs. He wanted them not to worry about these needs once He had left them. He reminded them of God's great care for them – greater even than the care God had for the birds who are well provided for. He reminded them that worrying about something that God is in control of is pointless. God has our days numbered, so surely He has also planned how our needs will be met, right?

Worry is often a battle of the mind between truth and the unknown future. The truth is, that God cares for us more than we can imagine, He is in control of everything, and worrying achieves nothing except distracting us from Jesus. The unknown future, which our minds worry about, is, well, 'unknown' and therefore at the mercy of our imagination.

▼ *more...*

Finally, brothers, whatever is true, whatever is honourable, whatever is just, whatever is pure, whatever is lovely, whatever is commendable, if there is any excellence, if there is anything worthy of praise, think about these things.

—Philippians 4:8

The Bible tells us that instead of worrying about the unknown future, we should think thoughts that are true, honourable, just, pure, lovely, commendable, excellent, and praiseworthy.

What did we Learn about Worry?

1. It distracts us from Jesus.

2. It is a sign that we are depending more on ourselves than on Jesus.

3. It is a sign that we need to humble ourselves before Jesus by casting our cares onto Him.

4. We tend to worry about things that may or may not happen, which we can't do anything about, but God is in control of all these things, and He loves us deeply.

5. We can cast our worries onto God because He cares for us.

6. We need to continually cast our cares onto Jesus, not just once, because sometimes our minds will be in the habit of 'taking back' those cares, just so we have something to worry about!

7. Worry does not add a single hour to our lives. It cannot change anything. But God can.

8. Instead of worrying, we need to think on what is true, honourable, just, pure, lovely, commendable, excellent and praiseworthy.

Study Questions

Finally, brothers, whatever is true, whatever is honourable, whatever is just, whatever is pure, whatever is lovely, whatever is commendable, if there is any excellence, if there is anything worthy of praise, think about these things.

—Philippians 4:8

1. If you were in the kitchen with Martha as she was preparing a meal for Jesus and you noticed she was getting more and more worried, how would you use Philippians 4:8 to encourage her to think on what is true. Use the following sentences to start you off.

   'Martha, I can see you are worried about serving the Lord today. Philippians 4:8 tells us how we are to think instead of worrying. Here are some things that are true for you about this situation ...'

2. Martha sees instantly that you are right! She says, 'Yes, I can see that the truth is I am 'doing' when I should be sitting at the Lord's feet and listening to Him! What should I do next?' What is your answer?

3. Martha takes your advice; she goes to the Lord and confesses that she was more concerned with doing for Him, rather than listening to Him. He forgives her and she sits down at His feet, her mind at peace and her ears open to listen to Him.

4. Martha finds you later because she has a question for you. 'I know that sitting at Jesus' feet is always the best option for us. But sometimes there are things that we need to do, and it's right

▼ *more...*

to do them, but still we worry about them. How should I think about them so that I guard my mind by thinking on things that are true and honourable and just and pure …?'

You think back to what you have learnt from the Bible about worry and decide to list off some of those things so she can guard her mind from worry. Jot them down on a piece of card, which you can keep handy for times you are tempted to worry.

5. Think about a situation that you are worried about now, or something that has worried you in the past. Using the advice you gave Martha, now write down the advice you would give yourself.

Let's Pray Together

Dear God, thank you for the lessons that the Bible has about worry. We see how being worried and anxious distracts us from Jesus, but we need Jesus more than anything. Please help us to guard our minds from worrying by thinking on things that are true, honourable, just, pure, lovely, commendable, excellent and praiseworthy. And in the times when we do worry, remind us to come and cast our anxieties on to you because you care for us. You are in control of all things. Please help us to trust in you for every part of our lives. Thank you for loving us so much that you even gave your Son Jesus that we might have forgiveness of our sins if we believe and put our trust in you. Amen.

MY ACTION PLAN ...

1.

2.

3.

4.

5.

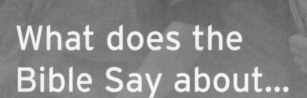

What does the Bible Say about...

Trials?

Think

Ask

Bible

The apostle Peter in the Bible is often described as 'the disciple with the foot-shaped mouth.' It's a crazy saying that means Peter often said the wrong thing, usually because he was hasty and didn't think before he spoke. Like the time he rebuked Jesus for saying that He was going to suffer and die. It seemed that Peter had forgotten that He was speaking with the Son of God, otherwise he would not have rebuked Him. It wasn't that he said, 'Oh Lord, I don't want that terrible thing to happen to you.' No, it was more like, 'I know better than you, this will not happen.' Peter was presuming to be wiser than Jesus by telling Him that He was wrong. Of course, Peter wasn't speaking this way to the Lord because he was being arrogant or unkind, but because he deeply loved his Lord and didn't wish to think of Him suffering and dying. However, Jesus in turn rebuked Peter severely:

> *From that time Jesus began to show his disciples that he must go to Jerusalem and suffer many things from the elders and chief priests and scribes, and be killed, and on the third day be raised. And Peter took him aside and began to rebuke him, saying, 'Far be it from you, Lord! This shall never happen to you.' But he turned and said to Peter, 'Get behind me, Satan! You are a hindrance to me. For you are not setting your mind on the things of God, but on the things of man.'*

—Matthew 16:21-23

Wow – to be called Satan by Jesus must have been devastating. But Jesus explains why. He didn't literally think that Peter was Satan at that moment. But He did mean that Peter's desires could be used by Satan to prevent salvation coming to the world through Jesus' death and resurrection. Peter was not thinking about God's purposes and His plan to rescue sinners by Jesus' death as payment for their sin. No, he was thinking as a man who desired peace, comfort and happiness in his physical life, instead of thinking of what was needed for eternal life. Peter had yet to learn that sometimes God uses trials and suffering to bear fruit that will have eternal value. What does that mean? Think about a vine growing along a fence, perhaps a grape vine. When winter comes and the vines are no longer producing fruit or even have any leaves, it's time for them to be pruned. The gardener comes along and cuts back a lot of the old, woody part of the vine. Why does he do that? Doesn't it ruin the grape vine? No, in fact it achieves the opposite. Getting rid of the old wood encourages new growth in spring and with the new growth comes an increased amount of fruit on the vine. That's a picture of what suffering can do to a person. Suffering is like pruning; it gets rid of things in our lives which stop us from growing spiritually. After being pruned through trials, we can grow and produce fruit of the spiritual kind. Peter was yet to learn this lesson, but it was to come to him in a severe way.

After Jesus had returned to heaven to be with His Father, the disciples were hard at work, preaching the Gospel and shepherding the flock (the church). Satan was also hard at work and persecution of Christians was common and horrific. Many Christians were killed for their faith. They were tortured and imprisoned.

Peter had a hard job ahead of him, not only to continue to preach the Word and share the gospel with those who didn't know Jesus, but also to encourage the Christians who were being persecuted. Times would have been frightening for these dear folks and the temptation to turn from their faith in order to have an easy life would have been in some of their minds. So Peter wrote the church a letter, explaining to them that the trials they were suffering were so that their faith might be tested and shown to be genuine:

... you have been grieved by various trials, so that the tested genuineness of your faith – more precious than gold that perishes though it is tested by fire – may be found to result in praise and glory and honour at the revelation of Jesus Christ.

—1 Peter 1:6-7

It makes sense, doesn't it? The most important thing about a person is whether they know Jesus Christ as their Lord and Saviour. To have the opportunity for faith to be tested and made sure is a good thing, even though it might be terribly difficult at the same time.

When my brothers and I were growing up, we had a large tree at the bottom of our garden. The people who lived there before us had begun to build a tree house, but had only got as far as putting up a few planks to make part of a floor. So my brothers and I spent many afternoons and weekends taking old bits of wood from the shed, along with Dad's hammer and a few handfuls of nails, and we did our best to complete the tree house. We did a pretty good job of making the floor and trying to get some walls and a bit of a roof. It looked pretty dodgy, but as the older sister I saw it as my job to make sure it was safe for 'my boys'. I would go up and put my full weight on the planks to test whether they were going to be strong enough to hold us. Thankfully they were because it was a pretty high drop. But you could liken my weight on the planks as the trial/test. The planks were able to hold my weight and so they passed the test, and then we were able to use the tree house for the purpose we had always wanted it for! To play in it!

About the same time that Peter was writing to Christians, his fellow apostle, James (the half brother of Jesus), was also writing to Christians about trials:

Count it all joy, my brothers when you meet trials of various kinds, for you know that the testing of your faith produces steadfastness. And let steadfastness have its full effect, that you may be perfect and complete, lacking in nothing.

—James 1:2-4

James points out a few things to us. I wonder if you can see them in the above verses. Look at the second half of verse two. '...when you meet trials of various kinds...' James is pointing out an obvious truth to us all. The word 'when' tells us that there will be trials in everyone's life; it's just a matter of 'when' and not 'if'. Trials are a part of life.

The next thing I see is that there will be trials of various kinds. We shouldn't be surprised when we encounter hard things in life, as the Bible warns us that they will come:

Beloved, do not be surprised at the fiery trial when it comes upon you to test you, as though something strange were happening to you. But rejoice insofar as you share Christ's sufferings, that you may also rejoice and be glad when his glory is revealed.

—1 Peter 4:12-13

Did You Know ...?

Peter was crucified for his faith, but he chose to be crucified upside down because he did not consider himself worthy to die as Jesus did. Peter died honouring Jesus.

James also writes of trials being a test. That the testing of our faith produces steadfastness (another word for this is endurance). But we need to be careful here – our response to the trial is key to steadfastness being produced. Look at the first four words in verse two. 'Count it all joy'. That perhaps sounds a bit odd, but count it all joy doesn't mean that we get all silly and giddy when a trial comes, like, 'Yipppeee, we're having a really hard thing happen in life!!' No, it's more a sense of thankfulness because of what the trial can produce in our lives. Trials are hard and they stretch us, sometimes causing us pain and heartache. But our response to the trial is the most important thing.

We can do one of two things. The first thing we can do is complain and grow bitter about it. We can look around us and think that no one else is struggling like we are and feel angry that God is allowing us to hurt. Do you think that this response will grow good spiritual fruit in our lives? No, it won't.

See to it that no one fails to obtain the grace of God; that no 'root of bitterness' springs up and causes trouble, and by it many become defiled.

—Hebrews 12:15

The verse in Hebrews warns us that bitterness can take root in our lives and will cause trouble, not only for us but for others too.

However, if we respond with joy, thanking the Lord for allowing a trial to test us, and ask Him to help us to bear it and to have the strength and wisdom to deal with it, we will see steadfastness of our faith in our lives. And others around us will see it too. We might wonder why it is so important for Christians to be steadfast. James answers that for us:

Blessed is the man who remains steadfast under trial, for when he has stood the test he will receive the crown of life, which God has promised to those who love him.

—James 1:12

Again, James is telling us just what Peter was saying: that those who remain steadfast (those who endure trial with the right attitude) will pass the test. We all love passing tests, don't we? This has to be the most important test we will ever face. The crown of life is eternal life. When we pass from this life, having endured all its trials and hard times, we will receive eternal life. Let's make one thing really clear, though. This is not about earning eternal life by enduring trials. Eternal life is not earned: it is only through faith in the Lord Jesus that we will have eternal life. No, James is writing to those who believe they are Christians, wanting them to see that trials enable them to make sure their faith is genuine.

When both Peter and James were writing these letters (which are now in our Bible), they were writing to Christians who were suffering persecution in ways that might be hard for you and I to even imagine possible. One way for these folks to avoid persecution was to recant (turn from) their faith in Christ. If they were to openly deny they were Christians, they wouldn't be persecuted. Only those who truly held their faith as the most precious thing they had, would refuse to deny Christ. So Peter and James were encouraging these dear folks, reminding them that though they might lose their lives, their eternal reward of life with Jesus was their ultimate goal. And it should be our ultimate goal too. There are terrible things that happen today to people, and even to Christians. But we who are truly saved need to be reminded that this world is not our home, so all that we might lose here is nothing compared to what we are to gain.

Of course, that does not mean we have a flippant attitude about suffering or trials, either in our own lives or in anyone else's life. You only need to look to Jesus to see His compassion for people who were in hard situations, to know that we also should respond in that way too.

So we have learnt some things about trials. But apart from responding with the right attitude, what else should we do?

Is anyone among you suffering? Let him pray.

—James 5:13

James tells us, we need to pray. Why should we pray?

God is our refuge and strength, a very present help in trouble.

—Psalm 46:1

God is the God who never sleeps, He never leaves those who are His. We can always go to God for help. Pray and keep praying in time of trial. Ask God to achieve His will in your life (Matthew 6:10), to help you endure the trial (1 Corinthians 10:13), to give you strength to persevere (Philippians 4:13).

But wait, there's more!

What other Principles can we Learn from Scripture?

On November 22nd, 1873 the Spafford family planned a special trip to England. They were all going to sail together from America and no doubt spent months organising suitcases, planning their itinerary and dreaming of all the wonderful adventures they would have together. The time came for them to depart but some unfinished business meant that Dad had to stay behind to care for that, while Mum and the four young daughters began the long journey. Not to worry, though; Dad would join them as soon as he could and then their adventures would really begin! But sadly the wonderful adventure-filled trip became a hideous nightmare for this whole family. As Mrs Spafford and her daughters sailed across the sea, their ship collided with another vessel and it rapidly sank. The

▼ *more...*

Spafford family became just husband and wife once more as their four daughters all drowned. Anna Spafford sent a telegram to her husband that began with these two words "Saved alone …'

Mr Spafford boarded a ship to join his grieving wife in England, sailing over the very place his daughters all lost their lives. During the journey, as his own heart broke with the sad reality that he would not see his daughters in this life again, he penned the words of one of the most beautiful hymns written. The hymn, which you might know, is called 'It is well with my soul.'

When peace, like a river, attendeth my way,
When sorrows like sea billows roll;
Whatever my lot, Thou hast taught me to say,
It is well, it is well with my soul.

(Refrain:) It is well (it is well),
with my soul (with my soul),
It is well, it is well with my soul.

Though Satan should buffet, though trials should come,
Let this blest assurance control,
That Christ hath regarded my helpless estate,
And hath shed His own blood for my soul.

My sin, oh the bliss of this glorious thought!
My sin, not in part but the whole,
Is nailed to the cross, and I bear it no more,
Praise the Lord, praise the Lord, O my soul!

▼ *more...*

For me, be it Christ, be it Christ hence to live:
If Jordan above me shall roll,
No pang shall be mine, for in death as in life
Thou wilt whisper Thy peace to my soul.

—Horatio G. Spafford, 1873

What we see in the words of the hymn that Mr Horatio Spafford wrote, is his firm belief that God is in control, which enabled him to say in the midst of even the most horrible, horrible times, 'It is well with my soul.'

Another way of saying 'God is in control' is to say 'God is sovereign'. You might think of royalty when you hear the word 'sovereign' and you would be correct. Sovereign means supreme ruler (king), and the king has complete control over all things that happen to anyone and anything. That describes God. We need to always remember that God is sovereign, even during times of trial in our lives. Just as Horatio Spafford could trust the Lord through his terrible trial, so too can we.

Look at the following verses, which speak of God's sovereignty.

The heart of a man plans his way, but the Lord establishes his steps.

—Proverbs 16:9

I know, O Lord that the way of man is not in himself, that it is not in man who walks to direct his steps.

—Jeremiah 10:23

Whatever the Lord pleases, he does, in heaven and on earth, in the seas and all deeps.

—Psalm 135:6

▼ *more...*

What did we Learn about Trials?

1. A trial is a time of suffering or challenge that can hurt us, discourage us and test us.

2. Trials come in many forms and they come to everyone.

3. Having the right attitude in a trial dictates how we will respond.

4. The Bible tells us that we are to choose joy in times of trial, because we will have opportunity for our faith to be shown as genuine.

5. God uses trials in our lives to grow us and mature us, bringing forth good fruit in our lives.

6. We need to be prayerful during trials.

7. We need to remember God is sovereign and we can trust Him in times of trials.

Study Questions

Know this, my beloved brothers: let every person be quick to hear, slow to speak, slow to anger; for the anger of man does not produce the righteousness of God. Therefore put away all filthiness and rampant wickedness and receive with meekness the implanted word, which is able to save your souls. But be doers of the word, and not hearers only, deceiving yourselves.

—James 1:19-22

▼ *more...*

1. The above verses in James follow after the encouragement for those in a trial. Why do you think James wanted to give out these instructions at the same time as speaking to them about trials?

2. When we are in a time of trial, we can be tempted to respond unwisely. We can become those who don't listen to wise advice, who speak and gossip about our trials and who caused them and we can become angry about our situation. Can you think of a time when you were struggling in a trial and you responded in this way? Perhaps something hard had happened at school or home? Why do you think that it's unwise to respond this way?

3. Quick, slow, slow. That's the advice James gives: Quick to listen. Slow to speak. Slow to become angry. Think about a trial you have experienced and how you could apply these wise principles to how you responded.

4. Verse twenty tells us why our response is so important. Write down your answer.

5. Verse twenty-one begins with 'Therefore'. It means 'because of what you have just read, now do this'. It tells us to put away all sinful responses, but it also tells us to do one other thing. What is that?

6. Receive with meekness the implanted Word. What does that mean? It means humbly receive the Word of God, which you know. Implanted tells of something planted within you. When we read the Word of God, His Word is planted in us. We are to humbly receive it (accept it and submit to it) because it brings salvation to us.

▼ *more...*

7. Give an example of what it might look like if someone was only a hearer of the Word, not a doer. Can you think of a time in your life when this has been you? Is there something in your life right now in which you need to become a doer and not just a hearer?

Let's Pray Together

Dear God, thank you for what the Bible teaches us about trials. The ultimate trial ever suffered was Jesus being separated from you in order to bear the penalty of our sin. Thank you for His example of willingly enduring that trial so that we didn't have to. Thank you that you never leave us in times of trial, but you are always with us. Please help us to be those who do your Word as we face hard circumstances. Help us to be thankful that you give us the opportunity to grow and mature. Please forgive us for the times we have complained. Help us to be those who patiently endure, constantly pray and rejoice in all circumstances. Amen.

MY ACTION PLAN ...

1.

2.

3.

4.

5.

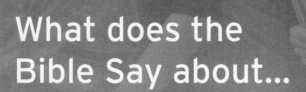

What does the
Bible Say about...

Family?

Think

Ask

Bible

The Book of Genesis provides a record of the very first family in human history, beginning with a man and a wife, followed by children. Very sadly, though, things did not go as they should have for this family. Some terrible tragedies occurred, and these tragedies have consequences for our own families today. Are you curious? Let's look together at the world's first ever family, way back in the beginning:

> Then God said, 'Let us make man in our image, after our likeness. And let them have dominion over the fish of the sea and over the birds of the heavens and over the livestock and over all the earth and over every creeping thing that creeps on the earth.'
>
> So God created man in his own image, in the image of God he created him; male and female he created them.
>
> And God blessed them. And God said to them 'Be fruitful and multiply and fill the earth and subdue it and have dominion over the fish of the sea and over the birds of the heavens and over every living thing that moves on the earth.'
>
> —Genesis 1:26-28

These verses from Genesis chapter one are from what we call the 'creation account'. It's the real life account of when God made the world and everything in it. It's amazing that we have a glimpse back to what happened thousands of years before we were even born, but it shows us that from the start God had a plan and a purpose for everything, including the family.

But before God made the family, He had to make humans, right? So this is a little snapshot of what happened when man was made. There are some interesting things that we can learn from these verses about the 'man' (humans) that God made.

The first is that God made humans in His own image. That means that God made us to reflect some of His own wonderful characteristics.

For example, God the Father is in perfect relationship with His Son, Jesus. John 1:1 tells us that Jesus (the Word) was with the Father from all eternity. They love one another deeply and when we read through the gospels we continue to see the loving relationship Jesus has with His Father. God made humans to love each other deeply and to thrive in relationship with each other. We see it in Genesis 2:18 when God said, *'It is not good that the man should be alone; I will make a helper fit for him.'* We enjoy relationships with family (and friends, classmates and neighbours …), but as we will soon see, because of sin we can never be in perfect relationship with each other in this life.

The second interesting thing we can see from Genesis 1:26-28 is that God established roles for humans, even from creation. What does that mean? Well, a role is a specific job for someone to do. For example the role of a teacher is to instil a love of learning in their students while helping them to learn. The role of a doctor is to serve their patients by doing all they can to help them to be well. We see in Genesis 1:26 that God gives humans the role of 'having dominion over' all of the animals and even the creeping things! That means to rule over. God made us the 'top dog' on earth, subject only to Him. We'll soon see that God has given humans roles in the family too.

The third interesting thing we can see is that after God created man and woman, He blessed them. When God created the world and all the wonderful things in it He said it was 'good' – I wonder if you would use a different word than just 'good' to describe creation. I would! Amazing! Beautiful! Inspiring! But God said it was good and it was. God saw man and woman as good too, but He also saw them as different to everything else He had just made. He wanted men and women to marry and to have children and form that family relationship which reflects the relationship we have with Him. This was part of the blessing that He gave.

We can see already that the verses in Genesis chapter one actually lay a foundation for family. So, who was this first family that God created? Their names were Adam and Eve. First, God made Adam and then, when He saw that it wasn't good for Adam to be alone, He made Eve out of one of Adam's ribs. She really was flesh of Adam's flesh and bone of his bone. Adam and Eve were married and became Mr and Mrs! God made Adam the head of the family, and to Eve He gave the role of being Adam's helper. That made them a great team!

God placed Adam and Eve as caretakers of the beautiful Garden of Eden, to enjoy and work and raise their family in. Can you imagine it? There were

Did You Know ...?

The name Eve means 'life'. God gave Eve the very special role of being the one who would bring life into the world through childbirth. What an honour for Eve!

crystal clear rivers that wound their way through the enormous gardens. There were lions, giraffes, sheep, cats, dogs and every other animal and creeping thing imaginable, all living peaceably together in the garden. There would have been trees of all shapes and sizes and colours, fruit and vegetables, plants and flowers, bees and warm sunshine—all theirs to enjoy as husband and wife.

Perhaps Adam and Eve swam each morning, hiked before lunch, played with the animals and dug in the warm soil in the late afternoon, while looking forward to the cool evenings when they would have walked through the garden with God. It must have been the most beautiful place because it was unmarred by the effects of sin and all its ugliness. But it would not remain like this for long. God gave Adam and Eve just one rule: They were not to eat the fruit from the tree of the knowledge of good and evil (Genesis 2:15-17). That doesn't seem too hard, does it? After all, the garden would have been full of good things to eat. However, Satan came to Eve in the form of a serpent and persuaded Eve to eat the fruit. Then she gave some to her husband to eat, so he did. Suddenly, their lives were changed. The first husband and wife had now committed the first sin. The relationship they had with God was broken. They hid themselves from God's presence when they heard His sound in the garden (Genesis 3:8).

But God, in His grace, provided animal skin coverings for Adam and Eve for their nakedness (which was a symbol of God's forgiveness of their sin).

Then Adam and Eve had to leave the beautiful garden, which had been their first home. The presence of sin in their lives now meant that pain, sickness and death became a part of their lives and indeed the lives of every human ever to be born from that moment on. But God continued to show His love and blessing to Adam and Eve. Soon they became a family of three as a son joined them, followed by another son later.

So there we have it, the first ever family. Dad, Mum and two children. But what happens next?

> *In the course of time Cain brought to the Lord an offering of the fruit of the ground, and Abel also brought of the firstborn of his flock and of their fat portions. And the Lord had regard for Abel and his offering, but for Cain and his offering he had no regard. So Cain was very angry, and his face fell. The Lord said to Cain, 'Why are you angry, and why has your face fallen? If you do well, will you not be accepted? And if you do not do well, sin is crouching at the door. Its desire is for you, but you must rule over it.'*
>
> —Genesis 4:3-7

We can assume that God had instructed Adam and Eve to shed the blood of an innocent animal as a sin offering to Him. The above passage from

Genesis chapter four describes Cain and Abel bringing their offerings to the Lord. Cain's offering was not acceptable to the Lord and so the Lord spoke to Cain and counselled him to choose to do the right thing, which would be acceptable. Sadly, Cain's proud heart chose sin instead, of obedience. In his sin the second tragedy for this family occurred. Cain killed his brother Abel. Can you believe it? But keep reading because it gets worse:

> *Cain spoke to Abel his brother. And when they were in the field, Cain rose up against his brother Abel and killed him. Then the Lord said to Cain, 'Where is Abel your brother?' He said, 'I do not know; am I my brother's keeper?'*

—Genesis 4:8-9

Cain lied to the Lord. Of course the Lord knew what had happened to Abel but He was giving Cain the opportunity to confess his sin and repent (turn) from it. Sadly, once again, Cain chose sin. God had no choice but to send Cain away from his family and his home.

I think it is easy for us to imagine that when the Bible speaks of family, it speaks of a perfect dad and a perfect mum with perfectly obedient and cheerful children. Is that what we have seen here with the first ever family? Absolutely not, although I am sure there were some happy times together in amongst the terrible. But overall what we have seen is a very sad and tragic account of a family. And I suppose that there is much about this family that we can all relate to.

Today, no matter how hard we looked, we would not be able to find one perfect family anywhere in the world. All of us sin, and sin destroys and hurts us. Perhaps you are already thinking about an argument that you had with a brother or sister, or perhaps even with your mum or dad. Yes, sin messes up families, but we always have the opportunity to ask the Lord for forgiveness and His help.

Sometimes sad and terrible things happen in our families. When Adam and Eve sinned, relationships between man and God and with each other changed. At times we think we know best – just like Eve did in the garden when she chose to eat the forbidden fruit. And perhaps the choices we make will have horrible consequences that affect the whole family. And then some families are affected by the consequences of Adam and Eve's sin. Sickness and death hurt families. There are many things that can hurt, challenge or even destroy a family, but in every circumstance, God reaches out to us and offers us hope.

What is that hope? The hope is that regardless of how wonderful our family is, or how hard it is sometimes to be in our family, there is always a place for us in God's family. God's family? Yes! If we believe in Jesus Christ as our Lord and Saviour and repent of our sins, Jesus saves us and we become children of God. John 1:12 says, 'But to all who did receive him, who believed in his name, he gave the right to become children of God.' Are you a member of God's family?

What did we Learn about Family?

- God created family as part of His beautiful creation.

- The relationships that we have with each other are because God created us in His image – with the ability to love one another deeply.

- God uses families to meet our need for companionship.

 more...

- God places children in families to be loved and nurtured.

- Families have a wonderful opportunity to teach children about the Lord.

- Sin has meant that families are not and will never be perfect, but there is always hope for individuals and for families as a whole.

- God has provided a way for everyone to be a part of His family – through His Son Jesus.

But wait, there's more!

What other Principles can we Learn from Scripture?

Bible

King David's son Solomon was the wisest man on earth. When he became king, God told Solomon to ask for whatever he desired and it would be his. Instead of asking for great wealth or a greater kingdom, Solomon asked God for wisdom that he might govern and lead the people well. God made Solomon the wisest king in all history. King Solomon wrote most of the book of Proverbs in the Bible and he addressed it to his son. It was almost like an instruction manual for life. Let's look at just a few of those wise words Solomon wrote and see what we can take to apply to family life.

My son, do not forget my teaching, but let your heart keep my commandments, for length of days and years of life and peace they will add to you.

▼ *more...*

Let not steadfast love and faithfulness forsake you; bind them round your neck; write them on the tablet of your heart. So you will find favour and good success in the sight of God and man.

Trust in the Lord with all your heart, and do not lean on your own understanding. In all your ways acknowledge him, and he will make straight your paths. Be not wise in your own eyes; fear the LORD and turn away from evil. It will be healing to your flesh and refreshment to your bones.

Honour the LORD with your wealth and with the firstfruits of all your produce; then your barns will be filled with plenty and your vats will be bursting with wine.

My son, do not despise the LORD's discipline or be weary of his reproof for the LORD reproves him whom he loves, as a father the son in whom he delights.

—Proverbs 3:1-12

Study Questions

1. Adam and Eve didn't have Scripture to study, but we do. When you read Proverbs 3:1-12, what do you think Adam and Eve did not do?

2. Why do you say that?

3. Which of the Proverbs would apply to Cain's behaviour?

4. Why do you say that?

5. Verses 3-10 are commandments with a promise. Write out each command and below it write the promise in a different colour. Can you see that obedience to God brings blessing?

▼ *more...*

6. The above Scripture from Proverbs seems like great wisdom for families. Which of the verses do you see as especially important for families today? Why?

7. There are so many other principles in Scripture that we can apply to the family and how we are to treat each other. Look up the following verses and write out the principle for families to follow:

   Matthew 22:37-39; Romans 12:1-4; Colossians 3:12-17; Ephesians 6:1.

8. Write out some things that you have learnt that you can be/do in your family to promote love and peace. Spend some time in prayer before the Lord asking for His help, and if you need to, make sure you confess any sin if you have done things that have not promoted love and peace in your family.

Let's Pray Together

Dear God, thank you for your Word, the Bible, which gives us so much help and wisdom. Thank you for the principles that I can learn and the examples that I can see of family life. Lord I know that sin has meant that families sometimes are not what they ought to be, but please help me to be a blessing in my family. Use me for your glory and give my parents the help they need. Lord, I want to pray as Solomon instructed, that the (insert your family name) family would trust in you with all our hearts, and not lean on our own understanding. May we acknowledge you in all our ways so that you would make straight our paths. May we not be wise in our own eyes but may we fear you and turn from evil. Thank you for my family. Amen.

TRUST IN THE LORD WITH ALL YOUR HEART, AND DO NOT LEAN ON YOUR OWN UNDERSTANDING. IN ALL YOUR WAYS ACKNOWLEDGE HIM, AND HE WILL MAKE STRAIGHT YOUR PATHS. BE NOT WISE IN YOUR OWN EYES; FEAR THE LORD AND TURN AWAY FROM EVIL. IT WILL BE HEALING TO YOUR FLESH AND REFRESHMENT TO YOUR BONES. (PROVERBS 3:5-8)

MY ACTION PLAN ...

1.

2.

3.

4.

5.

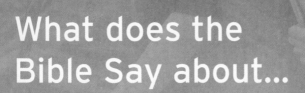

What does the
Bible Say about...

Grief?

Think

Ask

Bible

Once upon a time there was a family who were healthy, happy and blessed. In this family was a man, his wife, their three daughters and seven sons. The man was very wealthy; he had many animals (a sign of great wealth in his culture) and many servants. He was a righteous man who loved God, and in fact he was known by others as 'the greatest man in the East.' His name was Job and you can read all about him as he has a book in the Old Testament of the Bible named after him.

Job's life sounds pretty amazing, doesn't it? Well, it was. Job had a large family around him, more wealth than he needed and a reputation of greatness in his country. He was seriously blessed. Every day his children would feast together, enjoying one another's company, until one day tragedy occurred. As his sons and daughters were feasting, a great wind blew, causing the house to collapse on them all. There were no survivors. It gets worse. All of Job's servants and animals were killed also. You might be wondering how all of these terrible things have happened in one day. You need to read Job chapter one to understand that the devil was testing Job's faithfulness to God by taking away all that was dear to him. God allowed the devil to do this, knowing that Job was truly a righteous man. And yet, God knew this would hurt Job terribly. We might be tempted to wonder why God would allow this to happen in Job's life, but a little later on we will see the importance of making sure that our faith is genuine.

[A servant speaking to Job] 'Your sons and daughters were eating and drinking wine in their oldest brother's house, and behold, a great wind came across the wilderness and struck the four corners of the house, and it fell upon the young people, and they are dead, and I alone have escaped to tell you.' Then Job arose and tore his robe and shaved his head and fell on the ground and worshipped. And he said, 'Naked I came from my mother's womb, and naked shall I return. The

Lord gave, and the Lord has taken away; blessed be the name of the Lord.' In all this Job did not sin or charge God with wrong.

—Job 1:18b-22

This is horrific. What a terrible thing to happen. Job's behaviour showed his great grief.

Did You Know ...?

Job's actions seem strange to us, but tearing his clothes and shaving his head were expressions of grief common to his culture.

Perhaps you are wondering 'what is grief?' Grief is the way we respond when we have lost someone or something very dear to us. Everyone responds differently to loss: some people will cry, some will be silent. Some people want time on their own, some people hate to be on their own. Some people want to talk about their loss, some people can't bring themselves to talk about it. We are all different.

Job expressed his deep sadness by tearing his clothes and shaving his head. Is it okay that he did that? Absolutely it is. The Bible even says that in his actions this man did not sin. Wait – am I saying that it is possible to behave sinfully in our grief? Yes, that's right. It is possible that we could sin as we express grief and sadness. We'll look a little more at that soon.

First, let's look at Job a little more. We saw Job's response to the terrible news. But we missed one important detail. Look back at those verses again and see if you can pick it out.

Job heard the news, he tore his robe, he shaved his head, and he....
worshipped. That's right, he worshipped. Let's take a step back. Job
was a righteous man. He knew God. And because he knew God, he
understood some important truths about God which enabled him to
worship amidst perhaps the deepest trial he was ever to face. He was
expressing his trust in God, regardless of what God allowed to happen
in his life.

However, Job's wife struggled in her grief. She responded in a way
that speaks to us of anger and bitterness:

> *Then his wife said to him, 'Do you still hold fast your integrity? Curse
> God and die.' But he said to her, 'You speak as one of the foolish
> women would speak. Shall we receive good from God, and shall we
> not receive evil?' In all this Job did not sin with his lips.*
>
> —Job 2:9-10

Even in response to his wife's unkind words to him, Job responded to her
in a way that was wise, reminding her of truth. In some Bible translations
of Job 2:9-10, the word evil is translated adversity (meaning 'a difficult
situation'), which helps us better to understand what was meant. Job is
asking his wife, 'Should we just expect good things to happen to us all
the time and not hard or difficult things?'

Job asked his wife this question, again out of his own knowledge not
only of God but of himself. What do I mean by that? Job knew he was a
sinner. He knew that God in His mercy had provided salvation through
faith. In fact, it would seem that God had allowed Job to understand
that one day in the future, the Son of God would come to the earth
and pay the price for his sin. Job said, 'For I know that my Redeemer
lives, and at the last he will stand upon the earth. And after my skin has
been thus destroyed, yet in my flesh I shall see God' (Job 19:25-26). Job

knew that his sin separated him from a relationship with God and there was nothing that he could do to fix that. Job knew that he needed a REDEEMER.

Why did Job need a Redeemer to die to pay the penalty for his sin? Remember that *'the wages of sin is death, but the free gift of God is eternal life in Christ Jesus our Lord'* (Romans 6:23).

Job believed that his sins were paid for and forgiven by God. Christ would one day suffer and die on his behalf, and on the behalf of all sinners who come to trust in Jesus Christ because of his saving work on the cross. I believe. Do you?

Job's faith allowed him to understand that he deserved nothing good in his life because every good thing comes only from God. He knew that God did not owe him anything. In fact, he understood that God had given him everything. Do you believe this? God has given His one and only Son Jesus to die on the cross for the sin of the world (John 3:16).

And yet Job still grieved when this terrible thing happened to his family. Grief is normal and natural. In fact, grief is what we experience because we love deeply, just as God created us to. It is what we do when our hearts are breaking. If we were to read in John 11:35 we would see that even Jesus wept in grief at the death of his friend Lazarus.

There is much that we can learn from Job and how he grieved.

Then his wife said to him, 'Do you still hold fast your integrity? Curse God and die.'

—Job 2:9

Remember earlier that I said it was possible to sin in our grief. We saw that Job's wife responded differently to Job in her grief. In fact, not only was her response sinful, but it also provided a temptation for Job to sin too.

When we experience the death of a loved one, we might struggle to understand why God has allowed it to happen, and we certainly would wish that it hadn't happened. But it is wrong to curse God in our grief. Job knew that. Remember, Job knew that he deserved nothing from God, but in fact he had received everything in the gift of salvation from sin, through Jesus.

It is also wrong to do the second thing Job's wife did. Can you see it? She wished Job dead! Sometimes in times of grief it is tempting to be angry at those around us – often those who love us. But we need to guard our hearts from angry and hateful responses to others. Even in our grief, we are still called, as Christians, to exercise love and self-control.

Even so, there still might be times that we sin in our grief. We might lash out at those around us. We might want to be angry with God for allowing such horrible things to happen in our lives. Job certainly was.

What? You thought I said Job didn't sin in his grief. He didn't – initially. But after a while he did. He felt very sorry for himself and got very angry with God, accusing God of forsaking him. Then God responded to Job, and it wasn't pretty. He rebuked Job, reminding him just who he was talking to:

Then the Lord answered Job out of the whirlwind and said: 'Who is this that darkens counsel by words without knowledge? Dress for action like a man; I will question you, and you make it known to me. Where were you when I laid the foundation of the earth? Tell me, if you have understanding. Who determined its measurements- surely you know! Or who stretched the line upon it? On what were its bases sunk, or who laid its cornerstone, when the morning stars sang together and all the sons of God shouted for joy?'
                                                                    —Job 38:1-7

What we read in these verses is God reminding Job that he is a mere human. On the flipside, God also reminds Job of who He (God) is. These seven verses are by no means the end of God's rebuke of Job. In fact, God rebukes Job with the same kind of questioning for four chapters! Through rebuking Job, God is revealing more of Himself. He humbles Job, reminding him that He is the Almighty, all-powerful God of the universe. And Job's response? He repented:

> Then Job answered the LORD and said: 'I know that you can do all things, and that no purpose of yours can be thwarted. 'Who is this that hides counsel without knowledge?' Therefore I have uttered what I did not understand, things too wonderful for me, which I did not know. 'Hear, and I will speak; I will question you, and you make it known to me.' I had heard of you by the hearing of the ear, but now my eye sees you; therefore I despise myself, and repent in dust and ashes.'
>
> —Job 42:1-6

Job repented and God forgave him. Even in his brokenness and grief, Job knew that he had sinned against God with his complaints and accusations. Job realised that God was in complete control and that he could trust God's hand over his life. He also acknowledged that he could not understand God's purposes, but that God's purposes are wonderful even when we can't see it. And these important truths provide us comfort when we grieve too.

But wait, there's more!

What other Principles can we Learn from Scripture?

Bible

We read in Psalm 147 of God's great comfort to us in healing our broken hearts. God is a God of compassion to those who are His.

He heals the brokenhearted and binds up their wounds.

—Psalm 147:3

The book of Isaiah reminds us that God is our strength in times when our hearts feel overwhelmed by the hurt and grief.

Fear not, for I am with you; be not dismayed, for I am your God; I will strengthen you, I will help you, I will uphold you with my righteous right hand.

—Isaiah 41:10

We also read in the book of Thessalonians that Christians can grieve with hope. If our loved one who died was a Christian, we know we will see them again in heaven! What a wonderful reunion to look forward to. Heaven is a wonderful place, which the Bible tells us is a place of amazing beauty that God has prepared for us to live in! It's a place where there will be no more tears or sadness. Imagine the wonderful reunion with our loved ones, which can go on into eternity as we all worship the Lord together!

And if we aren't sure if our loved one was a Christian, we are still to grieve with hope, because God is sovereign and only He knows the

▼ *more...*

heart of a man or woman. Remember how the thief on the cross next to Jesus got saved just before he died? Grieve with hope, trusting that God does what is right and good.

> But we do not want you to be uninformed, brothers, about those who are asleep [have died], that you might not grieve as others do who have no hope. For since we believe that Jesus died and rose again, even so, through Jesus, God will bring with him those who have fallen asleep. For this we declare to you by a word from the Lord, that we who are alive, who are left until the coming of the Lord, will not precede those who have fallen asleep. For the Lord himself will descend from heaven with a cry of command, with the voice of an archangel, and with the sound of the trumpet of God. And the dead in Christ will rise first. Then we who are alive, who are left, will be caught up together with them in the clouds to meet the Lord in the air, and so we will always be with the Lord. *18 Therefore encourage one another with these words.*
>
> —1 Thessalonians 4:13-18

Grief is one of the hardest things that we have to deal with in our lives. To have someone we love, no longer be with us is heartbreaking. But there is one more thing I want to remind you of: this life is not forever. When Adam and Eve were in the garden of Eden, they chose to disobey God, which changed forever how our physical lives would be. Their choice to sin caused death to become a reality for every person born since, because the penalty of sin is death. That sounds depressing, doesn't it? But we need to remember that death is not the end. God promises that all those who believe in Jesus as their Lord and Saviour and repent of their sin, will know life not only on this earth, but in heaven with Him!

What did we Learn about Grief?

Ask

1. Grief is what we experience when someone we love dies.

2. God is in control of all that happens in our lives.

3. It is right to express grief emotions, as long as we are not hurting others or cursing God.

4. Everyone is different in how they express grief.

5. It is possible to sin in our expression of grief, but God is quick to forgive when we are sorry.

6. Grief is a part of this life because of death. Death is the penalty of sin. But death is not the end. Jesus promises eternal life with Him to all who repent of their sin and believe in Him.

7. God comforts Christians who grieve by healing broken hearts.

8. God strengthens us as we grieve.

9. Christians can grieve with hope, knowing that all Christians will be reunited and live together with the Lord.

10. We can grieve trusting God, knowing that only He knows the heart of man.

Study Questions

A young couple, Jim and Elisabeth Elliot, went as missionaries to Ecuador to reach the Auca tribe with the gospel. Sadly, Jim was killed by some of the Auca men, leaving behind his young wife and daughter. As you can imagine, Elisabeth's heart was broken. And yet, even in her intense grief she chose to trust God in this severe trial and she set out to reach this tribe of people herself. Elisabeth knew that God was God. In other words, God is free to do what is best in His eyes because He is God and He knows all. Elisabeth would never have chosen for her young husband to die, but through his death many people, including a number of the Auca tribe, came to believe in the Lord Jesus as their Saviour. Elisabeth said these words:

'God is God. Because He is God, He is worthy of my trust and obedience. I will find rest nowhere but in His holy will that is unspeakably beyond my largest notions of what He is up to."

— Elisabeth Elliot

1. Elizabeth Elliot understood that God has a right to allow things to happen in our lives to achieve His will and purposes. Sometimes we don't understand straight away what His will and purposes are and sometimes we never will. In reading Elizabeth's words above, what was it that made her trust God in such a terrible situation?

2. 'God is God' – what does that mean?

3. Why is God worthy of our trust and obedience? What has He done in order to make Elizabeth say that? What verses can you think of to show that?

4. Why was Elizabeth able to find 'rest' in God's holy will? Was it because she didn't care about what had happened? Or was it that she trusted God completely, even if it meant that she would suffer?

5. The following Scripture reminds us what to do when we suffer. *'Is anyone among you suffering? Let him pray.'* (James 5: 13).

Elizabeth Elliot was a woman who knew that her strength and help would come from God during her intense time of suffering. She cried out to the Lord in prayer. Do you need to pray right now for God's strength, help and comfort? Or is there someone you know who is grieving who you can pray for? Take some time to pray.

Let's Pray Together

Dear God, even in the depths of sorrow, you know how our hearts suffer. We read of the Lord's tears at the death of Lazarus and we are so thankful that you are a God of love and compassion. Death is one of the hard things in life for us to understand, but you have promised to be our comfort, strength and help. Lord, when we grieve, we ask for your help. Protect us from the temptation to grieve selfishly, to not love others and to reject you, but instead help us to cling to you in times of sorrow and distress. May we be as Elizabeth Elliot, who trusted you and honoured you in her grief. Thank you for the hope that you provide all Christians. What a wonderful promise believers have! They will be with you forever, in heaven, a place where there is only joy, no tears or sadness. Thank you that it is the gospel that provides us with such hope. Amen.

HE HEALS THE BROKENHEARTED AND BINDS UP THEIR WOUNDS. (PSALM 147:3)

FEAR NOT, FOR I AM WITH YOU; BE NOT DISMAYED, FOR I AM YOUR GOD; I WILL STRENGTHEN YOU, I WILL HELP YOU, I WILL UPHOLD YOU WITH MY RIGHTEOUS RIGHT HAND. (ISAIAH 41:10)

MY ACTION PLAN ...

1.

2.

3.

4.

5.

What does the
Bible Say about...

Attitudes?

Think

Ask

Bible

I wonder what you know about a guy in the Bible who was swallowed by a big fish? Do you know who I am talking about? Yes, it's Jonah. What else do you know about Jonah?

Let's see … well, he was living in Israel and he was a prophet. God told Jonah that he needed to go to Nineveh and tell the people there to repent or they would all be destroyed. But Jonah didn't go to Nineveh; instead, he jumped on a ship and headed for Tarshish. God sent a raging storm after Jonah and each crew member cried out to his god for mercy. After the crew cast lots and found out that Jonah was responsible for the storm, Jonah knew that crying out to God for mercy was not what he needed to do. Jonah told the crew to throw him overboard and they would be saved. Eventually, though reluctantly, they did and the seas became calm. But what happened to Jonah? He was swallowed whole by a huge fish, where he spent three days and nights. That's a lot of time in the belly of a fish. A lot of time to think and reflect on his attitudes and behaviour. Was Jonah repentant? It seems he was. Jonah's prayer from inside the fish tells us that he cried out to the Lord and the Lord answered his prayer. The fish vomited Jonah up onto dry land and God gave Jonah a second chance to obey and go to Nineveh. This time, he obeyed.

That should be the end of Jonah's story, right? After all, there's the happy ending we all wanted. Jonah obeyed God and headed to Nineveh to carry out his role as a prophet, just as he should have when God first told him. It all worked out well in the end. Except it didn't. Outwardly Jonah was obedient, but in his heart there was still a big problem.

Let's give a little bit of background to Jonah's problem. We know that Jonah was an Israelite and that he was a prophet. If you were to read through the Old Testament you would see that Israel, God's chosen people, were often unfaithful to God. They had times when they walked with God, obeying His commands and seeking to do His will. But more often than not, the Israelites chose to turn their backs on God and live life without Him. Then life would get hard and the Israelites would cry out to God for forgiveness and mercy, and God, in His loving kindness, would intervene and help His people. But it wouldn't be long until the Israelites were too comfortable once more and they would turn their backs on God again. The book of Judges illustrates this common cycle. In the time of Jonah, the Israelites were not walking with the Lord.

> ## Did You Know ...?
> *A prophet was someone chosen by God to communicate God's message to the people. Some prophets wrote, and some spoke the messages.*

The other thing you need to remember is that Israel had enemies. Some enemies were vicious and ruthless. Nineveh was not in Israel. It was the capital of Assyria and the Assyrians were enemies of Israel. So there were a number of factors for Jonah: Israel hated Assyria, and probably they were scared of this nation too. Jonah would also have feared for his life amongst this ruthless people, but fearing for his life was not really Jonah's problem. Let's look further at what happens and you'll see exactly what was going on in Jonah's heart.

Jonah heads into Nineveh and calls out to the people, telling them of the destruction that would come in forty days if they do not repent. What happens?

The word reached the king of Nineveh, and he arose from his throne, removed his robe, covered himself in sackcloth, and sat in ashes. And he issued a proclamation and published it through Nineveh, 'By the decree of the king and his nobles: Let neither man nor beast, herd nor flock, taste anything. Let them not feed or drink water, but let them be covered in sackcloth, and let them call out mightily to God. Let everyone turn from his evil way and from the violence that is in his hands. Who knows? God may turn and relent and turn from his fierce anger, so that we may not perish. When God saw what they did, how they turned from their evil way, God relented of the disaster that he had said he would do to them, and he did not do it.

—Jonah 3:6-10

Wow! The people repented of their evil ways and were saved. The Bible indicates that there were at least 120,000 people in Nineveh at the time. Jonah must have been overjoyed! Imagine it: after a horrific experience in the belly of a fish, he heads to Nineveh where the people are known to hate Israelites, and not only does the king listen and heed the call to repentance, but he orders everyone else to bow their hearts to the true God as well. God used Jonah in an amazing way. A whole city was saved and transformed! And Jonah ... well, here's the problem. Jonah wasn't overjoyed. In fact, he was angry. Come and see ...

When God saw what they did, how they turned from their evil ways, God relented of the disaster that he had said he would do to them, and he did not do it.

But it displeased Jonah exceedingly, and he was angry. And he prayed to the Lord and said, 'O LORD, is not this what I said when I was yet in my country? That is why I made haste to flee to Tarshish; for I knew that you are a gracious God and merciful, slow to anger and abounding in steadfast love, and relenting from disaster. Therefore now, O LORD, please take my life from me, for it is better for me to die than to live.'

And the Lord said, 'Do you do well to be angry?'

—Jonah 3:10–4:4

Jonah had a sinful attitude. A man of God, chosen to be a prophet – the one who brings the good news of repentance and salvation, the one who himself had benefitted from God's gracious gift of salvation – well, he was angry that the Ninevites had been saved.

What on earth is going on with that? Sure, the Ninevites were enemies of Israel but here was God, rich in mercy extending grace towards these hostile and violent people. They received God's mercy gratefully, and no doubt this news spread like wildfire, which made them an example to the, as yet, unrepentant Israelites. Shouldn't Jonah have rejoiced in this? Perhaps he should have hoped that his own people would look at what the Lord was doing amongst the Ninevites and want the same for themselves? But he didn't. Jonah, in his prayer after the Ninevites repented, exposed the attitudes of his heart to God and to us.

What is both interesting and very sad is that Jonah's own attitudes were the exact opposite to the very ways in which Jonah described God. Jonah described God as gracious, merciful, slow to anger, abounding in love and relenting from disaster. Doesn't that sound just like God? But sadly, it doesn't sound just like Jonah. What attitudes were in Jonah's heart? The Bible doesn't tell us – but we could probably guess:

- *Arrogance.* Jonah thought he knew better than God. He wouldn't have saved the Ninevites and he was angry that God did!

- *Selfishness.* Jonah was not willing for the Ninevites to have what he himself enjoyed, the free gift of salvation! Not only did Jonah enjoy it, he acknowledged that salvation belonged to God and was God's to give—but it seemed that Jonah did not really believe that it was God's gift to give to whomever He pleased.

- *Hatefulness.* Jonah expressed the worst form of hate that anyone could express: a desire to withhold salvation from people is the exact opposite of what God would want.

- *Indulgence.* Jonah indulged his belief that he should have his own way. When you indulge in sinful attitudes, you convince yourself that you deserve your own way so that when you don't get it, you believe you have the right to then be angry.

- *Anger.* When Jonah didn't get his own way, he became angry at God.

These are some examples of the attitudes Jonah nurtured in his heart. You might wonder how I can guess at these when the Bible doesn't tell us. The Bible tells gives us the answer:

No temptation has overtaken you that is not common to man. God is faithful, and he will not let you be tempted beyond your ability, but with the temptation he will also provide the way of escape, that you may be able to endure it.

—1 Corinthians 10:13

There is no sin that is not common to every one of us. I bet that you, just like me, could look through the above list and recognise some of those attitudes in your own life at times. Perhaps there have been times when someone has irritated you by not playing a game the way you think it should be played. Or when Mum or Dad has said 'No' to something you really wanted. Or perhaps you have just felt grumpy for no particular reason, but you believe you have the right to be sullen towards your family members just because that's how you feel.

But it doesn't have to be that way. We don't have to fall prey to sinful attitudes that seem so easy for us to slip into. God offers hope. He always offers us hope. The second half of verse thirteen speaks of a way of escape. Every temptation that we face will have a different escape route but we always have the ability, with God's help, to flee from temptation, to pray and focus our minds where they need to be and to reach out and ask for help from those who love us. Remember, sin is something we all struggle with. Here's another verse you might have already thought of yourself.

For all have sinned and fall short of the glory of God.

—Romans 3:23

All of us are sinners, and even those of us who are Christians will still sin, just like Jonah. Attitudes can be some of those sneaky sins in our lives. Sometimes they start small and grow and grow until we are changed and twisted by them. Sometimes we can hide them away in our hearts, not allowing anyone to see them. But if, like Jonah, we indulge our sin and hide it away in our hearts, supposing that no one can see (forgetting that God sees everything), we risk becoming hard hearted towards God and others. I wonder if you know of any attitudes in your heart that you need to deal with right now? Let me encourage you to pray, confessing to the Lord any attitudes that you need His forgiveness for and asking Him to help you not to indulge sinful attitudes in your heart.

But wait, there's more!

What other Principles can we Learn from Scripture?

Bible

Do you remember the story of Martha? She was the sister of Mary and they were both sisters of Lazarus, the man Jesus raised from the dead. They were also friends of Jesus. Let's look at Martha's story once again.

▼ *more...*

Now as they went on their way, Jesus entered a village. And a woman named Martha welcomed him into her house. And she had a sister called Mary, who sat at the Lord's feet and listened to his teaching. But Martha was distracted with much serving. And she went up to him and said, 'Lord, do you not care that my sister has left me to serve alone? Tell her to help me.' But the Lord answered her, 'Martha, Martha, you are anxious and troubled about many things, but one thing is necessary. Mary has chosen the good portion, which will not be taken from her.'

—Luke 10: 38-42

Martha was anxious and troubled. What causes us to be anxious and troubled? Anxiety comes when we replace the truth about God with our own thoughts. For example, Martha was worried about getting enough food made and served to her guests. The truth was that the Lord Jesus could have provided all that they all needed and more, while Martha could have joined Mary in listening to Jesus. Instead, Martha was telling herself that it was her responsibility to ensure everyone had enough to eat.

Here's another example. Martha became cross with her sister for not helping her in the kitchen. What was the truth in this situation? The truth was that Mary had chosen the best thing – sitting at Jesus' feet to hear what He had to say to her was food for Mary's soul! But Martha thought her way was the right way. She wanted Mary to join her in the kitchen to work preparing food. When she didn't get her own way, Martha became angry at her sister and rude to Jesus, ordering Him to tell her sister Mary to come and help her! Mary's attitude of wanting to humbly learn from Jesus was definitely the best option!

▼ *more...*

What did we Learn about Attitudes?

Ask

- Everyone is faced with the temptation to harbour sinful attitudes.

- Sinful attitudes need to be dealt with and not indulged.

- Sinful attitudes can cause our hearts to grow hard towards God and others.

- Sinful attitudes can make us unwilling to serve God.

- Sinful attitudes cause us to dishonour God.

- God provides a way of escape from the temptation of sinful attitudes.

- God always forgives those who repent of sinful attitudes.

Study Questions

Think

1. Martha asked the Lord a significant question. She said, 'Lord, do you not care?' Often we can think this in our own hearts when we start to indulge in a sinful attitude. We can become jealous of what someone else has or does and the more we think of it, the more we feel like we deserve it. Before we know it, our attitude is, 'Lord do you not care that I don't have/do that?' We become angry, self focussed and even rude to those around us. Can you think of a time when you have allowed an attitude to make you think in this way? What happened?

▼ more...

2. Martha's attitude of anger towards her sister was sinful. Martha chose to serve a meal to her guests and Mary chose to sit with Jesus. But when Martha realised the job she had taken on was too big and overwhelming, she became angry with her sister for not helping. How could Martha have dealt with this situation, instead of becoming angry with her sister?

3. Martha could have asked for help from the Lord in the provision of the meal for her guests. After all, He had already provided for thousands of people through the loaves and fish from a boy's lunch box. Sometimes our pride causes us to want to do big/important/hard things/things that will impress others, but then we are tempted to feel that no one else is as good/hard working/brave/selfless as us. What truth can we tell ourselves when we are tempted by the attitude of pride/self-importance?

4. Read the following verses and circle all of the attitudes that you see.

Put on then, as God's chosen ones, holy and beloved, compassionate hearts, kindness, humility, meekness, and patience, bearing with one another and, if one has a complaint against another, forgiving each other; as the Lord has forgiven you, so you also must forgive. And above all these put on love, which binds everything together in perfect harmony. And let the peace of Christ rule in your hearts, to which indeed you were called in one body. And be thankful. Let the word of Christ dwell in you richly, teaching and admonishing one another in all wisdom, singing psalms and hymns and spiritual songs, with thankfulness in your hearts to God. And whatever you do, in word or deed, do everything in the name of the Lord Jesus, giving thanks to God the Father through him.

—Colossians 3:12-17

▼ *more...*

5. Verse seventeen gives us a clue towards developing consistent attitudes that honour God. What is the clue?

   What is one way you can practice thankfulness this week?

6. Write out these verses in your journal or on a piece of card, and if you don't know the meaning of some of these attitudes, look them up in the dictionary. Choose one or two right attitudes each week for the next month or two and spend time asking the Lord to help you develop these attitudes in your life.

Let's Pray Together

Dear God, thank you for what we have learnt about attitudes. Thank you for exposing the attitudes in our hearts, like you did to Jonah, so that we can deal with them. Please help us to grow more like Jesus in our attitudes - to be selfless, loving and kind. Help us to be quick to repent of attitudes that dishonour you and hurt others. Amen.

FOR ALL HAVE SINNED AND FALL SHORT OF THE GLORY OF GOD. (ROMANS 3:23)

MY ACTION PLAN ...

1.

2.

3.

4.

5.

What does the
Bible Say about...

Our Bodies?

 Think

 Ask

 Bible

I am a New Zealander. That means I come from a country called New Zealand, in the South Pacific. Perhaps you know a thing or two about New Zealand. You might know it's almost at the bottom of the world. You might even know that *The Lord of the Rings* movies were filmed there, and that New Zealand has more sheep than people (yes, it's true). But the most important thing to know about New Zealand is that we have—in my opinion—the world's best rugby team. Of course, you may not know what rugby is – it's a sport. But to most New Zealanders, seeing our rugby team (the All Blacks) come onto the field and perform the *haka* (a war dance before the game starts) will bring us to tears when we are away from our home country. It's almost a part of who we are as a culture. It sounds extreme, but it's true. We just love it. Why? Because in our country of just over four million people, we have eleven young men who can beat any team in the world. We, the underdog (the ones who should be losing), are in fact usually the champions. What is not to love about that?

> Did You Know …?
>
> *When we touch something we send a message to our brain at 124 miles per hour!*

It's the dream of many school boys to become an All Black, and every Saturday morning throughout winter, thousands of parents stand on the side-lines in the freezing rain to cheer on their boy, who no doubt, dreams of wearing the black shirt in front of millions of people. But rugby is a hard game. It can cause serious injuries and damage to the body of even the professionals. But every rugby player would say that it's worth it, to sacrifice their bodies to the dream of playing for their country. So day after day, month after month, these guys are out on the field, training, running, kicking, tackling, pushing themselves harder and harder. They take their bodies to the very peak of athletic performance.

Our bodies are amazing! We can train them to excel in sports, dance, athletics, art, music. We can endure all sorts of terrible injuries and conditions for the sake of achievement. Again another New Zealander comes to mind as I think of Sir Edmund Hilary, one of the first mountaineers to reach the summit of Mount Everest, in 1953.

But not all of us are going to achieve great things on the sports field, or the mountain top, or the piano or the dance floor. In fact, most of us are going to battle to drag our bodies out of bed and into the shower each morning. So, how does that work? How is it that some people seem to be able to leap out of bed and onto the front page of the sports news, while some of us … just don't?

Actually, it has little to do with our body and more to do with our mind. We get out of bed early because… we choose to go to bed early, to set the alarm and to actually get up when it goes off. It's not that some people are born with an ability to get up when the alarm goes off, and some people just aren't. What we do with our bodies is all about choice.

We have the choice of how to use our bodies. Do we use our bodies for serving ourselves and our own purposes? Or do we choose to use our bodies to serve and glorify the Lord? That seems like a hard question. And perhaps we find ourselves wondering if there is a list of activities that fit the category of 'serving the Lord'? Let's find out.

Eric Liddell was a young Scottish man to whom God had given a great athletic ability. He could run very fast. In fact, Eric won the men's 400m race at the 1924 Olympics. But Eric was not like many of our athletes today. He was not a superstar. He did not want the attention or fame. He was not in it to make money. Nor was he prideful about his incredible speed. He said, 'God made me fast. And when I run, I feel His pleasure.'[1] Eric knew that he was made for God's own glory, and that God was glorified when he ran. We might think that running hardly seems

1. www.goodreads.com/author/quotes/802465.Eric_Liddell

like a 'spiritual' kind of activity, but the Bible guides us on this kind of thinking.

So, whether you eat or drink, or whatever you do, do all to the glory of God.
—*1 Corinthians 10:31*

Whatever it is we do, we can do it to the glory of God. How do we do that? Remember, it's not the actual activity that we are doing, it's the heart attitude behind it. We do all things to the glory of God when our attitude is of desiring to honour God. Eric Liddell ran for the glory of God, not because he was seeking fame for himself, but because he wanted to give glory to the Lord in all he did.

Eric Liddell was passionate about those who did not know Jesus as their Saviour. He said, 'We are all missionaries. Wherever we go we either bring people nearer to Christ or we repel them from Christ.'[2] He knew that he was a representative of Jesus – both when he ran and when he lived his day to day life. So Eric knew he had to use his body to serve Jesus at all times, regardless of what he was doing. He wanted to be someone who brought people nearer to Christ by how he lived. So he turned down an opportunity to run an Olympic race (for his best event) because it was on a Sunday and he wanted to keep Sunday as the day he met with other believers to worship the Lord. Even though he was ridiculed for it, Eric stuck to his decision because the Lord was more important to him than an Olympic medal or the opinion of others. The headlines in the papers around the world had a field day over Eric's decision – and still Eric did not budge. God was honoured in Eric's life in this decision.

There is someone else who knew that he had to use his body to serve Jesus. His name was Stephen. Stephen was a mighty man of God and he spoke boldly, telling people of Jesus and their need for Him as their Saviour. Sadly, though, there were some who did not want Stephen to be doing this, and so they trumped up some false charges and had him arrested.

2. www.goodreads.com/author/quotes/802465.Eric_Liddell

Stephen went to trial, and during the trial he took the opportunity to tell the people about Jesus. This infuriated the men, and they grabbed him and dragged him out of the city to kill him! They picked up rocks and threw them hard at Stephen to stone him to death. Even as those rocks were striking his head, his stomach, his face and his legs, Stephen continued to boldly proclaim the name of the Lord, until his body could take no more and he passed from this life to be with the Lord forever:

Then they cast him [Stephen] out of the city and stoned him. And the witnesses laid down their garments at the feet of a young man named Saul. And as they were stoning Stephen, he called out, 'Lord Jesus, receive my spirit.' And falling to his knees he cried out with a loud voice, 'Lord, do not hold this sin against them.' And when he had said this, he fell asleep.

And Saul approved of his execution.

And there arose on that day a great persecution against the church in Jerusalem, and they were scattered throughout the regions of Judea and Samaria, except the apostles. Devout men buried Stephen and made great lamentation over him. But Saul was ravaging the church, and entering house after house, he dragged off men and women and committed them to prison.

—Acts 7:58–8:3

It's hard to imagine how we would respond in such a situation, isn't it? Our natural instinct would be to fight to protect ourselves, and scream and cry out in pain. But Stephen did not do that. Stephen knew something that these hateful people did not know:

'I tell you, my friends, do not fear those who kill the body, and after that have nothing more that they can do.'

—Luke 12:4

Stephen knew that the body was only a person's shell. Life does not stop at physical death. For the person who believes in the Lord Jesus, life continues on in heaven with Him for all eternity. This earthly life was of little value to Stephen, compared to what was to come, and this knowledge enabled Stephen to use his body for the Lord! Do you see what Eric Liddell and Stephen have in common? They both loved the Lord Jesus as their Saviour. That alone caused them to make sure that whatever they did with their bodies, and therefore their lives, was for the glory of God and not of themselves. I wonder, is this something that is in your mind, and in my mind, as we choose how we will use our bodies?

But wait, there's more!

What other Principles can we Learn from Scripture?

Meanwhile, at the terrible scene of Stephen's death, we get a glimpse of someone who was not using his body to glorify the Lord. We have our first introduction to Saul. Saul was a Pharisee. You might remember that a Pharisee was a religious leader, but more often than not, their religion was false. As a young man Saul was a very zealous Pharisee. This means he gave himself 110 per cent to the role of being a Pharisee. Saul was especially committed to the cause of getting rid of Christians. As Stephen passed from this life, Saul accelerated his efforts in persecuting Christians. Saul was using his body for evil.

However, not too long passed before Saul was radically saved from his life of sin, and became as zealous a Christian as he had been a Pharisee! And to mark his new life in Christ, Saul received a new

▼ more...

name and became Paul. Now, with the Lord's purposes in mind, Paul went forward and used his body to glorify the Lord, preaching the gospel, planting churches and loving God's people.

Perhaps this idea of glorifying the Lord with your body is new to you, or maybe it's not but you've never really understood how it applies to you.

Let's see what David thought. Read some of Psalm 139 below, which he wrote:

For you formed my inward parts; you knitted me together in my mother's womb. I praise you, for I am fearfully and wonderfully made. Wonderful are your works, my soul knows it very well.

—Psalm 139:13-14

David knew God had made him and so he praised God! He said that we are fearfully and wonderfully made. That means that everything about us has been hand-chosen for us by God! He chose which family traits you would inherit – maybe you have your mama's eyes, or your daddy's nose, or your grandmother's way with plants! All of these things were chosen for you, so be glad you are exactly how God wanted you to be!

But how does being thankful for how we were made work in today's culture? You've probably noticed that the world around us is very focussed on bodies. It tempts us to be discontented with the way we look. 'If only I was taller, or my nose was cuter, or my eyes were blue, or my teeth were straight, or I was a certain size' – this is how the culture around us wants us to think. What does the Bible say about that?

▼ *more...*

But who are you, O man, to answer back to God? Will what is moulded say to its moulder, 'Why have you made me like this?' Has the potter no right over the clay, to make out of the same lump one vessel for honourable use and another for dishonourable use?

—Romans 9:20-21

Do you understand what these verses in Romans are saying? They are saying that we have no right to complain about our bodies. It is as if a pot would say to the potter, 'You've made a terrible job of me. You should have made me like that pot over there!' The idea of a pot speaking to a potter is ridiculous, isn't it? Well, that's also what the Bible says about us arguing with God over how he made us – it's ridiculous!

It's a very sad thing, but there are many who have fallen into the trap of believing that their bodies are not good enough. They believe that to be popular or successful, they need to look a certain way, and so they chase after that certain look, regardless of the cost to them or their bodies. This isn't new. It's been happening for hundreds of years…

Let's head back to China in the tenth century. The Chinese people believed that a tiny foot was a sign of beauty and wealth. So they did something drastic and crazy. It was called 'foot binding'. The foot binding would start in girls around four years old. Their toes would be tucked under their foot until they broke, and then they would be bandaged tightly in order to stop the foot from growing anymore. You can imagine that this would be terribly painful. It was also terribly dangerous because these injuries could lead to infections

▼ *more…*

that might even cost the girl her life. Parents would pay for people called foot binders to come to the house to break their daughters' toes and foot bones, and bind up the feet to keep them tiny.

You might think this fashion example is a little extreme. Well, it is. And there is a word for it. It's called idolatry. Do you know what that means? It means that the status symbol of a tiny foot had become an idol in the Chinese culture. What is an idol? An idol is the thing in our lives that is more important to us than anything else, and we believe that we can't be happy without it. It becomes the thing we worship.

In the Chinese culture, tiny feet had become a nationwide idol – even though to us it seems such a terrible and silly thing to do. But let's look back at our own culture today. Are there people in our own culture who are willing to do extreme and even dangerous things to their bodies because if they don't, they think they can't be happy? Yes, there are. It is an easy trap to fall into – the trap that has us making an idol out of our body. But here is what Scripture says to us:

For where your treasure is, there your heart will be also.

—Matthew 6:21

The verse in Matthew tells us that our treasure is whatever is the most important thing to us. It will often occupy the majority of our thoughts, and our behaviours and attitudes will be dedicated to it. For example, if we spend much of our time concerned with how we look, or improving how we look, we can safely assume that is what our treasure is. But Paul (otherwise known as Saul) has something else to say about this in the following verses:

▼ *more...*

> *I appeal to you therefore, brothers, by the mercies of God, to present your bodies as a living sacrifice, holy and acceptable to God, which is your spiritual act of worship. Do not be conformed to this world, but be transformed by the renewal of your mind, that by testing you may be able to discern what is the will of God, what is good and acceptable and perfect.*
>
> —Romans 12:1-2

Remember that when he was Saul, Paul had used his body for wicked purposes. But God took Saul and opened his eyes to the evil that he had been using his body for. Paul understood we can either serve the selfish ambitions of our bodies or we can use our bodies for selfless ambition. In Romans 12, Paul gives us a few things to think about.

1. Our bodies (as Christians) are to be presented to God as a living sacrifice, which is holy and acceptable.

   This means that we are to dedicate our bodies to the service of God (not the service of ourselves or our culture). Does this mean that we are to pack our suitcase and head to Africa as a missionary? Well, not right now, anyway! The Lord may have that in your future, but He may not either. He might call you to stay right where you are. But wherever we are, we are to present ourselves to God, willing and ready to be used by Him and for Him. That can only be done when our hearts are focussed on Him – not on our bodies. Don't allow how you look, or what you can do, to become a distraction from glorifying and serving the Lord.

2. To dedicate our bodies to the Lord is worship.

   Did you know that worship is not just singing praise to the Lord at church? Worship is honouring God in every activity of every

▼ *more...*

day. If we are living for the Lord, whatever we are doing (school, playing, music lessons, sports practice, baking, ballet, riding our bikes, etc) we are worshipping God. But we worship the thing that we treasure. Make sure that you are treasuring the Lord – not your body, nor the activities you choose for your body to do.

3. The opposite of offering our bodies as a living sacrifice is to allow our minds to be persuaded by the world's thinking about our bodies. But God transforms us by the renewing of our minds, which enables us to serve Him with our bodies.

   Remember to fight back the world's lies with truth, because this is the renewing of your mind. 'I am fearfully and wonderfully made! I am glorifying God with my body, I will not glorify myself.' 'It does not honour God when I use my body to gain attention for myself, and it is not an act of worship.'

5. Having a renewed mind enables us to test/prove/know God's perfect will for our lives.

   The will of God for any Christian is to honour Him with their lives. That sounds pretty easy, doesn't it? But as you have read, we are up against some tough opposition. Remember, it all starts with our minds. Every temptation to use our bodies for our own selfish purposes begins with one wrong thought – which we feed until it becomes all consuming. Remember what Paul said about not being conformed to this world, but instead renewing your mind? Renew – it means get rid of the old and put in the new. Get rid of those nasty old thoughts of serving your body and instead think of how you can glorify God.

   A little note of care … If you are tempted towards extreme measures in exercising or eating (or not eating) or other ways in

▼ *more...*

which you are trying to achieve a certain look or goal for your body – please, go to an adult, tell them what is happening and ask for help.

What did we Learn about our Bodies?

- God made us to glorify Him, not ourselves, with our bodies.
- We can glorify God in everything we do.
- God has made us. How our bodies are formed, how we look, the skills and strengths we have, are all good things which caused David to say that we are fearfully and wonderfully made.
- Our attitudes about our bodies and about God will decide if we glorify God or serve ourselves.
- We always have a choice about what we do with our bodies.
- The culture around us can distract us by tempting us towards being discontented with how we look, but we don't need to follow the culture.
- What we treasure, we will worship. Be careful of worshipping the body instead of God.
- God made us to be exactly who we are.

Study Questions

1. We can only glorify God with our bodies if we trust in Him as our Saviour. Do you?

2. What about your body, your skills, your talents and abilities, can you praise God for today?

▼ *more...*

3. How can you glorify God with the specific abilities and talents and body He has given you?

4. Have you been tempted towards being discontented with how your body looks or performs? In what ways?

5. Do you think you are influenced more by the world's views on our bodies and what we do with them, or by what the Bible teaches? How do you know?

6. How can you guard your mind from being influenced by the culture when it comes to thinking about your body?

7. What skills and/or abilities do you think you could develop to use in serving the Lord?

8. Read Psalm 139, David's response to God who made him. Write your own Psalm of response to God, who made you just as you are.

9. After reading this chapter, is there anything that makes you feel like you need to ask an adult for help? If yes, please do that as soon as you can. If it's something you find difficult to talk about, perhaps even ask them to read this chapter and then give them your answers to these questions.

Let's Pray Together

Dear God, you are my creator. You caused me to be born at the time you wanted me, in the place you wanted me to be. Thank you for the way in which you made me. Thank you that you have given me skills and abilities. Thank you for making me just the way you did. Please help me to serve you and glorify you with my body, my life, my attitudes and my time. Amen

MY ACTION PLAN ...

1.

2.

3.

4.

5.

LOOK OUT FOR
GOD'S WORD AND YOUR LIFE
by Laura Martin

ISBN: 978-1-78191-822-7

You've got a mind – use it! If you've got questions – ask them! But don't fill your mind with rubbish and it is important to ask the right questions. So how do you make sure that you're headed in the right direction? Well – *THINK, ASK – BIBLE! God's Word and Your Life* is the crucial ingredient. Read it – study it – learn it – think about it. God's Word will help you with your questions about social media, money and other exciting stuff like gaming, television, movies and even education! Find out about how Solomon, King Nebuchadnezzar, Mary and others experienced the same issues you do every day of your life – and how God is the same all-powerful God for you as He was for them.

Extra Features: Study Questions and Prayers

BY THE SAME AUTHOR

FOR GIRLS: LOVE IS

Do you think that sometimes the whole world seems to be singing about love – yet nobody really knows what it's all about? What is love? God is love. That's the answer. Based on 1 Corinthians 13, this book is a month's worth of daily readings and devotions on the theme of God's love.

ISBN: 978-1-84550-971-2

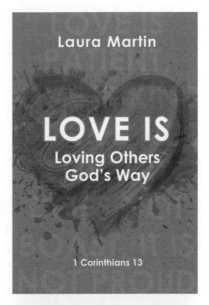

FOR BOYS: COMMANDED

Everywhere around us the clock is ticking. Everyone has a mission they are trying to achieve. If we are Christians, we have a mission of our own. Your mission is written in God's Word – the Bible. It is not all about you, though – it's about honouring God by the way you live.

ISBN: 9-781-78191-120-4

CHRISTIAN FOCUS PUBLICATIONS

Christian Focus Christian Heritage CF4K Mentor

Christian Focus Publications publishes books for adults and children under its four main imprints: Christian Focus, CF4K, Mentor and Christian Heritage. Our books reflect our conviction that God's Word is reliable and Jesus is the way to know him, and live for ever with him.

Our children's publication list includes a Sunday school curriculum that covers pre-school to early teens, and puzzle and activity books. We also publish personal and family devotional titles, biographies and inspirational stories that children will love.

If you are looking for quality Bible teaching for children then we have an excellent range of Bible stories and age-specific theological books.

From pre-school board books to teenage apologetics, we have it covered!

Find us at our web page:
www.christianfocus.com

CF4•K
Because you're never
too young to know Jesus